Insuring Success

Insuring Success

An Insurance Professional's Guide to Increased Sales, a More Rewarding Career, and an Enriched Life

Dan Weedin

GLOBAL
professional
publishing

Global Professional Publishing Ltd
Random Acres
Slip Mill Lane
Hawkhurst
Cranbrook
Kent TN18 5AD
Email: publishing@gppbooks.com

ISBN 978-1-909170-03-2

Printed by Integrated Books International (IBI)

Contents

Preface

Insurance was an accidental career for me. When I first came out of high school and entered college, I thought I would like to get into journalism. I became the sports editor of the college paper and tried to learn a little bit about radio. Sports radio was in its infancy and I saw myself as the next ESPN star. Then somewhere along the way, I decided that I would get into teaching high school History and coach basketball. Then I realized that teachers are woefully underpaid and, being newly married to my high school sweetheart, this didn't seem like a very good option.

My new wife Barb in an effort to support our ability to eat, got a job at a local independent agency in Seattle. I traveled there daily to pick her up after work and got to know some of the people. Through numerous discussions, I realized that insurance people weren't all that bad and you could make a legitimate career out of it. Next thing you know, I've applied for a job as a personal lines underwriter at an insurance company, got hired, and the rest is history. You will read about some of that "history" in the pages to follow.

Ironically in the 30 years after high school, many of my "dreams" did come true. I coached high school basketball for eight years (even got paid a little for it) and have been on local radio and television broadcasting sports. My current gig since 2004 has been as the stadium announcer for the high school football team. You just never know...

Insurance is a noble business and you should be a proud contributor to that. Many of you ended up in it "accidentally" just like me. And, like me you stayed in it. Many of you reading this have had years of success and some of you are just getting started. Regardless, the insurance industry is changing just like all other industries due to technology, communications, and the economy. If you're not prepared and ready to change, maneuver, and be nimble along with it, you could get swept away by the wave. If you choose to maximize your talents and take advantage of a tremendous time in our history (it always happens after a depression or recession – just watch), then you will realize the personal and professional rewards that an insurance career can provide. This book's objective (and my genuine reason for writing it) is to help you not only maximize that talent that you have, but to help you do it quickly.

Speed is king, so let's get sprinting!

Dan Weedin
Poulsbo, WA
January 2014

Dedication

I do have to acknowledge and thank several people who have helped me along the way. I won't bore you with everyone because that would take an awful lot of space, but here are my "greatest hits."

Thanks to my colleague and friend, Libby Wagner. Libby constantly cajoled and implored me to get a book written. I'm not sure I would have ever gotten started without her pestering me!

Thanks to my professional mentor, Alan Weiss. You will read much of Alan's wisdom that I've learned through working with him the past five years. He's the smartest person I know and literally brilliant when it comes to business and life. His generosity matches that. I am professionally where I am today because of his help and the community he created.

To my friends and colleagues in the community who helped me stayed focused on finishing this book – Noah Fleming, Jean Oursler, Roberta Matuson, and Gary Patterson – thank you!

If I didn't mention my kids in my first ever book, I'd be in trouble. Thanks to my daughters Mindy and Kelli for your love, support, and the various stories you've unwittingly allowed me to tell.

And all of this could not have been done without my lovely and adorable wife of over 27 years, Barb. She has been my rock and my guide and I am truly blessed to have her. I love her more than can be expressed in words.

And I guess my final thanks goes to you, the reader of this book. You've given me enough trust with your time and money to crack this open and see if you can learn a few new tricks and tactics. My sincere hope is that you walk away with strategies to help you both professionally and personally and that you thrive in your career and life.

Now, let's get busy!

About the Author

Dan Weedin founded Toro Consulting, Inc. in August of 2005. He works with insurance industry leaders to help them maximize their talents, enhance their careers, and enrich their lives. He has worked with countless insurance executives and principals across the country to grow them both professionally and personally.

Dan started his career in the insurance industry just two days out of college in 1987. After a brief stint as an underwriter at United Pacific Insurance, he became an award-winning multi-lines agent for two different independent agencies in Washington State. He was named Bell-Anderson Insurance Commercial Agent of the Year in 1992. He also earned the Federated Mutual Insurance Company Big Hitter Award four (4) times and was named to their Leadership Council four years in a row for excellence in sales and client retention.

Dan earned his Certified Insurance Counselor (CIC) designation in 1996 and completed his Certified Risk Manager (CRM) designation in 2011. He still holds his license as an agent and broker in the State of Washington; however he never sells insurance.

He has published numerous articles, op-ed columns, and executive briefs and has been quoted in several publications including the American Express OPEN Forum, *Insurance Journal, Best Review, Best Week, Independent Agent Magazine, US News & World Report, PIA Magazines, Toastmasters Magazine*, and the Society of Human Resource Management (SHRM).

Dan has been personally trained and whipped into shape by Alan Weiss to become one of Alan's "Master Mentors" in his global consulting community. He is one of less than 50 consultants in the world to hold that distinction. Dan was inducted into the Million Dollar Consultant™ Hall of Fame in 2012.

Dan is a faculty member for the Society of Certified Insurance Counselors providing continuing education training for agents on Commercial Property and Elements of Risk Management. He also speaks to groups and organizations on insurance and risk management related issues.

Dan is a graduate of the University of Washington where he received his Bachelor of Arts degree in History. You can say he fell into an "accidental career" in insurance! Dan is an active member of his community. He is a past president of the Poulsbo-North Kitsap Rotary Club, a member of Toastmasters, and is currently President of the board of directors for the North Kitsap School District. He is married to his high school sweetheart and they reside in Poulsbo, WA (near Seattle). He is the proud parent of two adult daughters. He enjoys playing golf, cooking gourmet burgers and duck tacos, and writing for his foodie blog. Most of all, he gains great enjoyment by being walked by his two canine bosses, Captain Jack and Bella.

Chapter 1

Volatility Exposed

Why insurance is needed more than ever, not less

As the world becomes more global and complex, ambiguity increases. As ambiguity increases, insurance becomes more crucial for financial and emotional protection, yet people don't know it. Insurance isn't simply a term or the commodity that so many companies have perpetuated through kooky advertising. It's a shared risk.

So as an insurance professional, why should you care?

That's a fair question to ask at the inception of this book. After all, you're about to make a decision whether reading this book is a good investment of your time. Trust me, it is. But not for the reasons you might think. Read on and you'll learn why.

Here is why you should care...

The stereotype of an insurance professional in North America isn't very flattering. Insurance agents rank somewhere in the cesspool that includes used car salesmen, sleazy lawyers, and graduates of the Willy Loman course on salesmanship. (Note: For those outside of the United States or those too young to have ever read or watched...Willy Loman is the central character of the Arthur Miller's American classic, *Death of a Salesman*. Pick it up and read it when you're done here.)

Don't try and convince me times have changed. The industry hasn't done itself too many favors over the past decade by playing down the role of the insurance professional, while accentuating the need to buy cheap insurance from people wearing a headset at any time of the day or night. Insurance has become commoditized, and the people who place that coverage (you) have become simply the people who sell it. You're not viewed as more important to the buying process than a vendor selling you a ham sandwich from a food truck.

If you're going to be regarded as a professional, as a trusted advisor, you need to be more than a salesperson that can offer the cheapest quote. You need to be an expert; someone that is willing to challenge beliefs and provide tough love; and someone that is astute about the history of their industry. If you don't know the "how and why" to the question of insurance, then you're just kidding around. If you commit to being educated on the origins and relevance of insurance, you're more likely to be able to adroitly carry your message, tell a story, and impact someone's life. And, oh yeah, you might actually be able to sell some insurance and make a career.

From the Ancient World to Cyberspace

This is the section you are probably considering skipping over, right? I can hear you grumbling – "Really? The origins of insurance? Yawn." Hang with me. I will make this painless and applicable to your job. I also promise at some point you will make a sale because you know it. Ready? Let's go...

> Many thanks to the Esurance web site with great information about the history of insurance. It's bookmarked on my desktop. Even though there is no intellectual property in telling the history, they did a terrific job of chronicling it and I want to give due credit to where I did my research.

In the Beginning – Think Gilligan's Island. That's right, the SS Minnow. What happened to the crew and passengers on that ill-fated trip? They got shipwrecked. Back around 3000 BC, this was a big concern for Chinese merchants. They grew weary of losing valuable merchandise in shipwrecks. Well before satellites, GPS, and reality television were available to find you anywhere in the world, the main peril for ancient businessmen was that their goods wouldn't get from Point A to Point B. So what they did was divide their goods evenly among ships, meaning that each boat carried a mix of cargo, not just on of any single merchant. You could say this was the beginning of diversification. It also meant a shared risk.

The Next Generation – About 1790 BC, the Babylonians tried something new. King Hammurabi put his stamp on insurance. He might be considered the first rich guy to throw his hat in the insurance ring. Let's call him the BC version of Warren Buffet! He suggested a concept called "bottomry," which allowed merchants to finance their shipping through loans from lenders. These loans were paid back with interest, only if the ship completed its voyage. If a peril took down the boat they were off the hook. Tell me if this sounds familiar – the merchants protected themselves financially for a premium? Hmmm.

The Middle Ages – Things didn't rock and roll as quickly back then as they do today. We are skipping a whole bunch of years because Steve Jobs and Bill Gates weren't around to accelerate the technology explosion. The very first insurance contract was signed in Genoa, Italy in 1343. The main business at that time was still cargo and merchandise being shipped places (we've always been a global economy, don't let anyone tell you differently). The theory behind this contract didn't differ from the Babylonians. Businessmen (merchants) would take out loans guaranteeing the safe passage and arrival of the valuable shipments. This time, however, we have a document (oh if they only knew what they started). This contract didn't include Coinsurance or Exclusions. We are still a few centuries away.

Fast Forward – We now find ourselves in 1666 and a new peril has arisen. It's one that won't go away through the next 350+ years. Fire. The Great Fire of London happened in this year, and it inspired the creation of the first fire insurance company. A guy named Nicholas Barbon founded this new-fangled insurance company. Mr. Barbon was an English economist, physician, and financial speculator. He was also only 26 years old when the Great Fire of London occurred. Although he helped pioneer and champion insurance as a business, his reconstruction work was done primarily for his own financial gain. Many insureds probably think nothing has changed!

The Damn Yankees – Benjamin Franklin was the best-known American businessman, philanthropist, author, and risk taker of his day. He became legendary. Mr. Franklin advanced the concept of fire insurance through his Philadelphia Contributionship in 1751. About 100 years later, insurance covering accident-related medical expenses reared its head (FillmoreCare for President Millard Fillmore? I don't think so). The Franklin Health Assurance Company of Massachusetts was the first United States insurance company to offer accident insurance for men who were injured in steamboat or railroad calamities.

Vroom, vroom. Hard to believe but the first car insurance policy was purchased well before Henry Ford started knocking out cars from Detroit. A guy by the name of Gilbert J. Loomis from Westfield, MA built his own car in 1897. As you can imagine, Mr. Loomis didn't have all the modern conveniences like rear-view mirrors and anti-lock brakes, so his day tripping around town was a peril for the horse and buggy set. He thought he needed a little risk transfer so he high-tailed it to the Lyman Agency and purchased a car insurance policy from (you guessed it) Travelers Insurance Company (you can't make this stuff up).

Over the next 30 years, cars quickly passed by the horse and buggy in the fast lane. In 1930, car accidents were killing 85 people per day in the United States. This opened the door for what you know today as auto liability insurance. Car insurance agents (like many of you) made their debut in 1934 and over the decades, the industry has grown with the accompanying needs.

Meeting Needs. Insurance started out protecting valuable goods for businessmen scared of losing it en route to its destination. Over the centuries, insurance always found a way to meet the needs of business. While concern over the exposures of transporting goods still is critical today (air, train, ground, ocean, cyberspace), business has many other issues that insurance protects:

- Property stored in buildings (and those buildings themselves)
- Liability created by the products, services, and transport of them
- Technology issues like cyber crime, loss of data, loss of power, connectivity, and reputation damage from social media (I'm guessing in 1900, the term social media meant a bunch of journalists out for a libation in a tavern)
- Continuation of business that's been suspended for some reason
- Consequences of natural disasters
- Intellectual property

Likewise, personal lines policies have become mandatory in many areas, and necessary in others. Protecting the loss of income due to death or disability; replacing property damaged by any number of perils; and protecting liability for damage to others are all part of this transformation to what originally was conceived centuries ago. As life grows and expands, so do our risks. As our risks expand, so does our desire to protect our lifestyle. Insurance, for all its detractors and those who banter and scoff at it, is the reason we as humans can go forth in life with peace of mind. It's a noble profession, and one that has been deemed to be of value dating back to a bunch of savvy business moguls in China many centuries ago.

As the world becomes more volatile, ambiguity increases

The world as it turns today is far more volatile than what our predecessors even 100 years ago faced. Let's consider the year 1914. From a personal perspective…

- Homes were smaller and simpler. Electricity, computerization, hot water heaters, and hot tubs weren't much of an issue. I am sure the term *smart house* would have drawn a wary glare from someone.
- Liability was less concerning. I'm pretty sure parties were held in 1914, but somebody falling down the steps after a third gin and tonic was

probably not going to sue you. Trespassers getting shot while trying to rob you wouldn't get their day in court. And, slipping on ice in front of your home was deemed to be the fault of the person with poor shoes and balance, not the homeowner.

- People didn't live as long. Life insurance policies were written for men only and men rarely lived deep into their 60s. Concern over paying for Junior's tuition at Harvard or Yale was not part of planning in those days for the majority of people. Being able to save enough to live into your 90s was folly.

From a business perspective…

- Globalization was centered on the country, not the world. What you did in Pittsburgh with steel didn't have any impact in China, Brazil, or India.
- Communications were much simpler. Emails, Internet, television, wireless, iPhones, etc. were never even contemplated. Heck, they didn't even know who Dick Tracy was back then! (Note – Dick Tracy is the super cool sleuth emerging in comic books in the 1930s. Dick had all the hippest gadgets like wrist radios, which are basically what smart phones are today)
- People were more concerned about fires damaging walls, not firewalls. They were more afraid of someone walking in and holding them up with a gun, rather than a kid they couldn't see robbing them blind sitting in his parent's basement.

I could go on and on. You get the picture. But let me make it even more real for you. In this century alone, volatility in our world has accelerated more than between 1914 and 1999 combined. Consider…

- In just the last 14 years, the Internet has gone from a curiosity to a critical business tool. Virtually every household is "virtual." That's not only true in North America, but globally.
- Email went from an afterthought to the worldwide default for business and personal communication. But wait, there's more. In the past 3 years, the increase in texting, Instant Messaging through a multitude of platforms, and visual communications like Skype, Face Time, and Google Hangout are reinventing communications. My guess is that in less than 10 years, Email will have gone the way of the typewriter.
- Technology has become a major exposure for business. The perils of theft, chaos, and loss of data will shut a business or organization down faster than any fire 15 years ago.

- There are more employees working virtually. Telecommuting has changed the landscape of "going to the office." As I am writing this book, I'm sitting comfortably at my home office with my dog Captain Jack "working" alongside me. I can reach anyone in the world with a touch of the SEND key, I can do virtual visual inspections and audits, and I can access and store documents without seeing an actual piece of paper. In 1999, I would have had to pay tens of thousands of dollars to do that, and probably would have had to rent office space. The significance of the autonomy and ambiguity of employees working from home cannot be underestimated.
- Reputations are more on the line than ever. You can't hide anymore. Business leaders are more scrutinized for what they say in public, what they do behind closed doors, whom they secretly email, and what they tweet (Twitter is the new business toy and tool. It doesn't give you the chance to say, "Oops!")
- Global business has more risk. The economic conditions in Europe, the advancement and competition from countries like China, India, and Brazil; differences in laws and cultures; and the necessity to achieve global market share have placed a ton of pressure on businesses both small and large.

Volatility is greater. Ambiguity goes even higher. As volatility increases, ambiguity doesn't stay proportionate. It creates a greater divide.

This is important to you because it means there is increased need for your expertise. The more ambiguous, the more questions, the more doubt, the more you are needed!

That means agents need to behave differently. They need to stop acting like a sales person and more like a trusted professional, a "must have" advisor. I don't care whether you're in commercial, personal, life, or ocean marine. Your credibility is the fact that you have "smarts" that aren't readily accessible elsewhere that will remove the fear caused by ambiguity. I know that's a mouthful, so check out the visual...

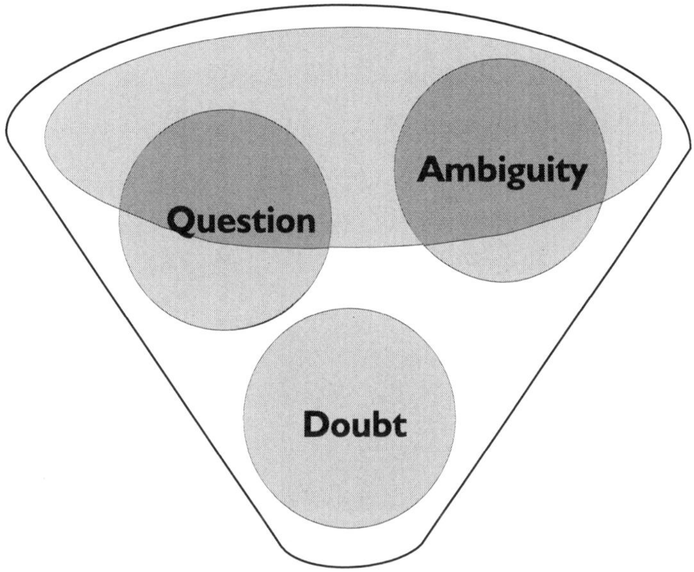

You are the answer

How do you behave or act differently you might ask. Here are my ***7 Simple Steps to creating insurance success in your career…***

1. **Stop cold calling.** You read that correctly. Stop cold calling. That's what door-to-door salesmen do. You might be more creative trying to use the phone or email, but the end result is the same. You have the look and feel of a sales person, and that rarely endears you. Don't get me wrong, sales is what makes business move. But sales are more frequent and more efficient when you are viewed as credible. (Chapter 5)

2. **Get more referrals.** This should be a daily routine to fill your prospect pipeline. (Chapter 6)

3. **Give away your value.** Write articles, blogs, and newsletters. Provide free resources. Host webinars. Create a professional web site with loads of great information.

4. **Dress like you're serious.** I know different areas and regions have different styles but that is never any excuse for not appearing professional. Business casual is fine in most places, yet too casual is unacceptable. You are all smart enough to know what I mean. To act like a pro, you need to dress like one.

Michael Jordan once was asked why he wore incredibly expensive suits when he traveled on road trips with the Chicago Bulls. After all teammates were often much more casual, and a few outrageous (see the Dennis Rodman years). Other than the fact he could afford it, Jordan had a great response. He said that he knew there were people for whom this would be the only time in their lives that they might see him in person. He wanted to make the best impression possible for those people. Enough said.

5. **Leave your technology in the car.** Really. The most I ever bring to a meeting is my iPad, and that is to take notes more efficiently. You do NOT need a slide presentation, fancy three-ring binders telling people about how great and wonderful you are, or a video montage of your life. Some of that is valuable on your web site or blog. That's where it belongs, not in your first meeting with a buyer. Bring a nice pen, a pad of paper, an iPad or notebook (if you're like me), a business card, and your brain. That's all you need.
6. **Stop talking.** Full disclosure…I've been guilty of this and sometimes still am. Most of the time, we "expressives" of the world get so excited and passionate about what we do that we talk over people and dominate a conversation. The more we allow the client or prospect to talk, and (this is an important 'and') we listen and stay in the moment, the more opportunities we get to find out how to most help them. The more we know that, the more likelihood we have of adding or retaining them as a client. Watch yourself on this one. You may need to have some self-governor. While at first it might seem like you're just gregarious, it can also be a huge turnoff and you will lose that credibility as an advisor.
7. **Do your research.** It's really not hard to learn about people and businesses anymore. The Internet provides you with various ways to do your homework and adequately prepare for a meeting. You will ask better questions; you will appear more professional; and you will stand out in the crowd amongst your competition.

Bottom line – The fact that insurance is becoming more complex, and increasingly needed, means that the world needs your smarts more than ever. They may just not realize it. Agents that appear to be slick and only about the sale will not look like trusted advisors. Those that implement my 7 Simple Steps will look and act the part, which engenders trust more quickly and translates into new clients and increased success.

Insurance is not just a term, it's a shared risk

From the beginning of this chapter, we have seen how ancient to modern day business professionals have used insurance as a shared risk. The issue is that the vast majority of your clients, regardless of their business acumen and sophistication, don't draw that conclusion readily. Why is that important you ask? Let's discuss...

One of my all-time favorite movies is *It's a Wonderful Life*, starring James Stewart and Donna Reed, and directed by the legendary Frank Capra. Mr. Stewart portrays George Bailey, a small town savings & loan president who goes through many personal and professional trials and tribulations down a road where he ultimately realizes he's had a "wonderful life."

There is a scene in the movie depicting a run on the bank during the Great Depression in the United States. All of his customers are clamoring wildly to get cash and want Bailey to cash in their savings accounts. Bailey has to explain to them that the money isn't in the bank...it's in each other's houses. I can still hear him now – "Don't you see? The money's not here. Why, your money's in Bill's home; and his is in Joe's; and his is in yours. And you all pay it back as you can..." The rest of the scene isn't as important. The concept is that all of the members of the savings & loan had basically bought into a "shared risk" concept, though they didn't fully understand that. They thought all their savings were stuffed into a bank vault, when the concept of suing it to build houses and gain interest is what made the bank, and them money.

Like the story above, your clients don't grasp the concept that their premiums go to pay for many things:

- Paying the for claims of other policy holders
- Paying to defend other policy holders
- Paying commission to the agent

- Paying for underwriting expenses
- Paying to build adequate reserves to keep the regulators happy
- Paying for all that spilt creamer in the break rooms

The most important for the purpose of this discussion is the first two bullet points. Understanding how shared risk works is important on several fronts.

1. It takes the concept of insurance out of the commodity way of thinking and into a more business oriented vantage point.
2. It emphasizes the importance of risk management, experience, and actuarial considerations. This means they get a clearer understanding of why insurance companies ask the questions they do during underwriting, and why they adjust claims in the manner they do.
3. It might have a humanizing effect. If people understood that their premium dollars are not solely going into the pockets of insurance agents and company executives, the ire created by increasing rates may be more muted. Heck, they may even start asking serious questions about company financial stability and loss ratios, rather than the price of the policy.

All the factors discussed in this chapter may on the surface seem superfluous. I'm glad you hung in there and read it. The reality is that the more you de-commoditize your product (an insurance policy) and help them understand the business concept (shared risk, shared reward), the more you reduce the sales label and increase your trusted advisor status.

Chapter 2
The Trinity

Why you need to understand the dynamic relationship among the players in an insurance transaction

Every insurance transaction involves three parties – the insurance company, the insurance agent or broker, and the insurance buyer. This little love triangle is more complex than it would seem. There is a significant difference between an "agent" and a "broker," and this difference is critical in how you deal with a prospect or client. It also makes a difference on how you are paid. The Trinity needs to be understood to properly leverage your client relationships; your carrier relationships; and your organizational sales process.

The insured

This is the insurance **buyer**. They are purchasing one or more insurance policies ranging from Personal to Commercial insurance; from Medical to Disability to Long-term Care; and from Life Insurance to Accidental Death Insurance. The buyer generally knows nothing about insurance, but is required in many cases to purchase it to protect their home, property, and business. They are often suspicious of the process and leery about the intentions of the person pitching them a policy.

The buyer is at a huge disadvantage. It's rare when the buyer of a product knows so little about it. When you buy a car, you've undoubtedly experienced driving one before. You know what it should and shouldn't do; you know how it will feel and look; and you normally have an idea of what you want.

Insurance is a mystery. It only gets triggered when something unpleasant happens. Too often, when it is used, there is an abundance of industry-speak, exclusions and contractual limitations, and wailing and gnashing of teeth. You now have a product with an equal parts mixture of calamity, acrimony, and frustration. The kicker is that the buyer still has to continue to pay for insurance for the rest of their lives at some level, and this only adds to the distastefulness of the entire process.

Any time you have an amalgamation of forced purchase for an intangible service that may or may not ever happen; when there is lack of clarity or faith; and when current events often portray the industry as a bunch of maroons, then the first side of the triangle is vulnerable and open to consternation and ambivalence. Not the way to embark on a beautiful relationship!

The insurer

The underwriter, the face, and the Darth Vader of the process. Just like a head coach in the National Football League, they take too much blame when things go wrong, and they get too little credit when things go well (claims paid, solutions realized, materials provided). In the direct writer world, the companies make the big splash and become *the brand*. Independent insurance companies tend to lie in the background and the local agent is the brand in the community they are located in. The company becomes a nameless monolith to where checks are directed. The insurer is the company of old that underwrote safe passage for ships. They will more often than not be the repositories of insurance information and the director of the process. They have the knowledge and are adept at making it known just exactly what they do know.

The agent

Here is where things can get a little dicey. Insurance agents work for the company or companies they are contractually obligated and bound to work with. Their relationship is stronger than the one with the insurance buyer. Contractually, the agent acts on behalf of the company and that's whom they represent. Their duty rests first and foremost with the company they are representing – NOT the insured. They get paid directly on commission from the company, so the insured never sees it. Brokers on the other hand don't have that contractual burden. Like a real estate broker, they work on behalf of the insured, their client. They also can charge an additional fee for their work to the client.

The dicey part is how an insured (and often an agent) gets this part mixed up. You will always hear agents talk to insureds and tell them how they represent them. That is not completely true. In addition, even though insureds know that their agents get paid, they have no idea how much. If you don't think this matters, think again.

What's in it for me – what's in it for you

Every relationship has a certain level of WIIFM (What's In It For Me). That's what makes personal and business relationships so tenuous, volatile, and downright scary at times!

What's in it for the insured: Peace of mind. Security. Lifestyle protection. Simplicity. Satisfying contractual obligations and requirements. You notice I didn't mention "cheap." People and businesses are willing to pay competitively priced premiums if their needs are met well. It's the insurance industry marketing geniuses who have educated people to be consumer shoppers and that price is king. It's not. They want the five things I mentioned at a competitive premium.

What's in it for the insurer: Profitable business. Although they genuinely care about the clients they serve, this is a bottom line industry. Shareholders and boards of directors are usually involved (mutual companies do exist, but they aren't non-profits!). If an insured all of a sudden becomes unprofitable due to claims, poor payment history, or an activity that is too risky for the insurer's appetite, they have no qualms with non-renewing that insured. If you've ever worked for a company, you know…insurers are about profit and seek clients that don't have claims.

What's in it for the agent: Reputation. Credibility. Financial stability. Most agents own or work for a small business. If you're a captive agent, an independent agent, or a specialist, you run a small business in a community. Your service and value proposition drive your existence. Your reputation is everything for long-term success and stability. You want to build a book of business that is profitable and be viewed as a trusted adviser in your community.

What's this mean?

As an agent or broker, you are the nexus of this trilogy. You are the glue that holds together the other two parties. You are the communication link, the one with all the answers, and the place that receives both praise and indignation.

Problems arise when communications break down between the insured and the insurer. This might be due to a claim dispute, a coverage interpretation, a non-renewal or cancellation letter, or bad publicity. (See AIG, Chartis, and back to AIG.) You have the ability to bridge that gap. Agents that are proficient in this skill thrive. Those that think they are good yet don't hold up to their own ethos lose clients for both themselves and their company carriers.

One other challenge for agency principals revolves around employees. Some employees excel at taking care of clients. Others, not so much. If the agency principal is not attentive to this, without knowing it they can be losing revenue, repute, and credibility.

Here are seven simple tactics you can take to help you continually bridge that gap and assure that all three parties in the insurance transaction are getting their just-deserved WIIFM:

1. **Train and educate internally.** I don't care how many employees you have, each and every one of them should receive some training on working with people. This seems to be taken for granted, yet is vital to good relationships. Please note, when I use the term "people," I also mean underwriters, claims adjusters, and company marketing representatives. Believe it or not, they are people, too!

2. **Be heady when it comes to understanding social styles and strengths.** One of the biggest mistakes agency principals make is to put people in roles that are ill suited for them. This takes discernment, discipline, and deftness on the agency owner's part. If you see disgruntled employees or complaining clients, you may guess that this might be at the root of the problem.

> My mother is a resident in a skilled memory care facility. The facility combines memory care with skilled nursing and assisted living, so it's a pretty big place. The receptionist at the front when you enter is named Melissa. Melissa is the perfect person to fill this role. She is always smiling, happy, gregarious, and self-confident. She memorized our names before my mom was officially a resident, and always called us by name when greeting or departing.
>
> One day, I learned from Melissa that due to a vacancy in another area, she was now transporting residents to doctor appointments and other events. Of course, she was outwardly cheerful and happy with the move. Here is the problem…Melissa was taken out of a role that she excelled in and (this is the important part) that made the resident's families feel welcome and valued. Now, the station was not manned as often, the people there are nice, but they do lack that unique gift of cheer that Melissa brought.

The family members are the actual clients, not so much the residents. Management missed the point. Anyone can drive a van. Not everyone can be a rock star as a receptionist and, the receptionist is the first and most important contact for any business. Never forget that.

3. **Never throw anyone under the bus.** This seems obvious, yet I think it happens more than you might imagine. It's awfully easy to paint the insurer as the "bad guy" to the insured. It might deflect acrimony from you to them. They are more faceless, so what's the harm, right? It is also easy to complain about an insured to the insurer, especially to underwriters and claims adjusters. While the sentiment may be true, you're not doing your client any favors.
4. **Be willing to fire clients and companies.** This seems to be counter to the whole goal of the insurance transaction, but bear with me. Not all clients are good clients simply because they can write you a check. If they cause undue burden to your staff, are not pleasant to deal with, are overly demanding, and actually lose you money then fire them. The size of the account doesn't matter. It's not worth the anxiety it causes to you, your staff, and your company carrier partner. Likewise, if you represent a company that offers you little support, mediocre or uncompetitive commissions or service, and you rarely use to place business, it's time to cut ties. It's better to move the small amount of business you have to companies that you are true partners with.
5. **Communicate early and often.** You may see this as a recurring theme in this book! I hear complaints from insureds that their agents don't call back or respond to emails quickly. Make a standard for responses. Tell your staff that all calls and emails (including to companies) are returned within 60 minutes. I can't imagine an agency office that with today's technology can't meet that standard. The worst hit to your credibility to both insured and insurer is poor *response management*.
6. **Be honest.** Again this appears so obvious, yet it's not entirely out of the realm of possibility that "little white lies" (or omissions) happen in communications. In a frantic effort to write new business, life agents may overlook the fact that someone that smokes a celebratory cigar 4-5 times a year and write them down as a "non-smoker." (Note – yes

I know some companies allow that…this is simply an example!) A commercial lines producer might omit telling a client that an audit on their revenue will be done at the end of the policy period and it could result in an additional premium. A personal lines agent may opt not to tell a prospect that a credit report will be required until after the policy has been issued. I know you're not naïve and know that these and even bigger gaffes occur all the time in this business. That's why you pay for Errors & Omissions coverage. Regardless, your culture should be one of complete honesty with insured and insurer. Part of this means educating your employees on the things they should be discussing with clients.

7. **Speed.** Like it or not, we live in an instant gratification world. This means communications, service work, issuance of policies and binders, and tests and reports that need to be completed. How quickly we issue good or bad news is important. Sitting on information rarely is in anyone's best interest. Getting out work rapidly is now a given. This speed of communications and workflow will markedly cut down on rancor between insured and insurer (and often you, too!).

Bottom line is that taking this transaction Trinity for granted is not in your best interest. I do understand this is only a small part of the process, and thus you see that this chapter is shorter than most. However the clever insurance professionals will use this knowledge to advance harmony between all parties. By successfully accomplishing this, the insured, the insurer, and the agent are far more likely to get what they want. The end result of that is less work, less stress, and improved profit for you.

Chapter 3

The Good Old Boy Finally Died

Profiling the new insurance professional

Sales is a relationship business. There is no argument on this point. Insurance is not only no different; it might be the poster child of relationship sales. The problem is that many producers have devolved into the equivalent of a used car salesman asking, "what will it take to get you into a new car today?" The objective needs to be to get insurance producers back into the relationship business by cultivating a culture of credibility and professionalism, rather than whom you play poker with on Saturday nights.

The proverbial "good old boy network" was all about relationships, right? It was about who knew whom and how well they knew them. The "network" was pretty strong. If you weren't in, then you had no chance of gaining an account. You got into the "network" by doing just that – networking. You bought drinks, you told stories, you told lies, you accepted others tall tales and yarns, and you played golf, cards, or whatever else was the game of choice. Even when I started in the business, the "good old boy network" was still alive and well. It was a game and you had to play it.

Being part of the "good old boy network" usually was reserved for portly, middle-aged white guys who hung around the same watering holes and stomping grounds. It was hard for the young, the female, and the non-Caucasians to break in. Some of you may scoff, but it was true. I had clients and prospects tell me as much. The good news is, that while relationships still do sell, the relationships aren't built on golf and beer, but on steak and sizzle.

This chapter is dedicated to burying the "good old boy" and leaving flowers on the grave. While "he" has been pretty much entombed for the past couple of decades, the way "he" went about acquiring business has been a legacy. The concept of wining and dining, spending money to impress, and being overly obsequious still exist. Don't get me wrong – showing your clients gratitude is just fine and you should do it. However, I've seen enough cases where the agent has spent more time on flattery than on making sure the insurance is up to snuff. In today's world, your client will drop you like a bad habit if you can't do the job on their most important protection. What that means is that your relationship has to be built on the strength of your skill and character, and by consistently delivering results.

Professional growth development – not just methodology

Let's do a little defining right now. *Methodology* in the insurance vernacular is the *how*. It's your technical skill, your ability to properly identify, program, and assess exposures, hazards, and perils. It's the real guts of the insurance process. Methodology is important, yet in the process of acquiring insurance it's only a part of the equation. This is a triune ingredient that is required to be truly effective at building relationships that result in new business…

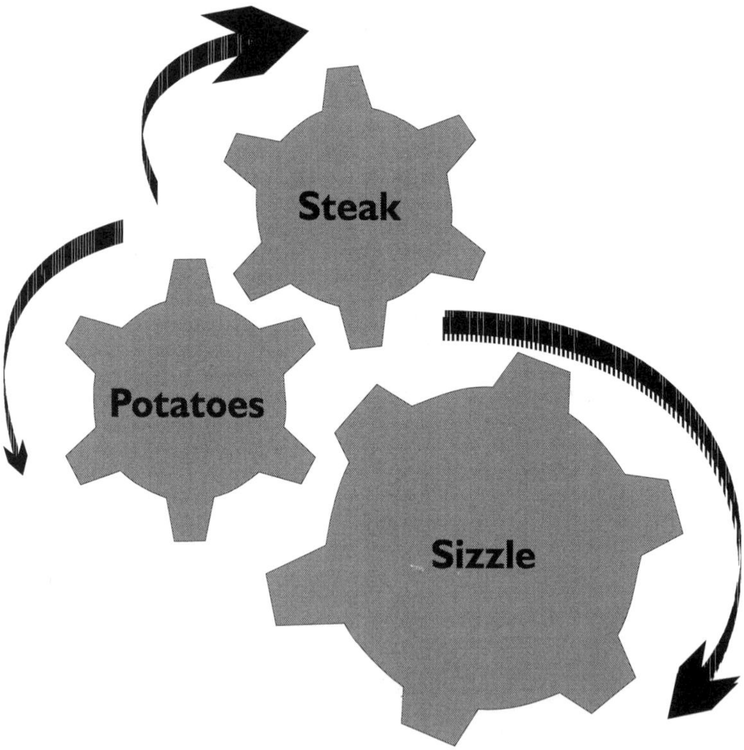

The Professional Growth Trinity

The "Steak" is *Communications*. In any fine dining establishment, steak is the heart of the feast; It is the flavor, the texture, and the body of the meal. Without a good steak at the core, everything else falls apart. (Apologies to all you vegetarians and vegans out there.) The same is true of the ability to communicate. This skill is more than simply the ability to open one's mouth and spew out words. Anyone can do that. However, the really sophisticated insurance professional has the capability of using several techniques to be truly persuasive and influential. Communications is a professional skill. It has to be taught, learned, practiced, failed, revised, and regurgitated until done well. Overlook this skill at your own peril. Here are my techniques to communication competency…

- **A substantial vocabulary** *and* the ability to use it adeptly, creatively, and in the right situations.
- **Timing.** The use of pauses and pace of the discourse are critical. I raised two daughters through the teenage years and coached high school girls' basketball for 6 years. Let me tell you, teenage girls can speak at breakneck speed. This is not the pace of play you want for a sales professional. Neither is the producer who languishes and bores the prospect before they even finish the first sentence. Communications is a skill, not an innate talent.
- **Confidence** is critical. When one lacks confidence and speaks, it's like watching a balloon slowly lose its air. You can tell by the pitch (too high means nervous), the trailing off, and the lack of conviction. When one communicates with confidence, there is a palpable sense of certitude from the listener.

  Watch the very best professional speakers in their craft. Regardless of your like or dislike for them, you have to give them their due. Speakers like Tony Robbins, Zig Ziglar, and Billy Graham are (or were) amazingly confident and that boldness spills over to the audience. Research shows that people will believe highly confident speakers, even if they are being less than genuine. Now I don't advocate anything other than honesty. My point is that confidence is king when it comes to speaking. You gain confidence from only one place. Practice. With practice will come small successes that over time build upon each other. There is no substitute or short cut.

- **Engagement.** This means eye contact, inflections, gestures, and facial expressions. I don't suggest you become an actor. I do advocate that you have to become so comfortable in your skin and with your ability that you are free to speak in the manner that you might at your Thanksgiving table with family and friends. If you can't engage your prospect and become an object of interest through your communication with them, you will never get the chance to seal the deal.

> **Shameless plug:** I have been a part of Toastmasters International for a decade. It is the best and most affordable place to learn to become a skilled speaker. It's a safe place to practice and fail; a safe place to get evaluated and gain suggestions for improvement; and the best place to develop extemporaneous speaking prowess. The last one may be the most important business skill you will ever have. Toastmasters clubs meet all over the world and are in almost any city or town. I encourage you to locate one near you and check it out at www.Toastmaster.org. Try a few out and join the one that most fits your schedule and open yourself up to grow. You will be happy you did.

The "Potatoes" is **Methodology**. The potatoes in the meal are the "glue." This may not sound appealing, but bear with me. The potatoes *ground* the meal. While not the "star" like the steak, they are highly important to the nutritional value and the consummation of the meal. With the insurance process, the methodology I described earlier in the chapter is the same thing.

You need to be credible as an insurance professional. That means you have to do all the work around understanding coverages, exclusions, benefits, and the like. You are expected to be the expert in the matter of insurance. This entails taking courses, keeping up with your continuing education, being knowledgeable about changes in the industry, and staying current with law changes.

The "Sizzle" is **Charisma**. There have been a lot of agents over time who have created a luxurious lifestyle for themselves based on this one factor alone. Charisma. It's defined in Webster's dictionary as *"attractive, enchanting, alluring, magnetic, and fascinating."* It's what makes you an object of interest. It's what gets you in the door, and often consummates a transaction. People who lack great charisma and have loads of methodology usually end up as actuaries and underwriters (nothing personal – just factual). People that have scads of charisma and want in proclivity to insurance knowledge end up writing business and getting "found out" shortly after. That business goes away. It's the people that have a balance of charisma, communications, and insurance smarts that end up sustaining a career.

People tend to think that charisma is innate; that you're either born with or without it. While it is true that for many, the strength of a charming nature is "built in" to you, that doesn't mean an introvert is doomed to spending their days anchored to a desk within a tiny cubicle. Charisma, like communications, is a skill.

To put a capper on this process, let's discuss how capable you need to be in these three areas. I believe you have the opportunity to be one of three things when it comes to offerings, services, and skills. I learned these from my coach and mentor, Alan Weiss, who is author of *Million Dollar Consulting*:

Competitive: Competitive means that you are as good as your competition. You offer similar company carriers, your services are equal, and your standards are the same. For example:

- Your office hours of 8:30 to 5:00 match your competitors. You don't have extended time frames, but you are competitive with others.
- You mail out a hard copy newsletter to clients. It's smart, well-written, and creative.
- You get your certificates of insurance sent out within 24 hours, not 24 seconds.
- You have a legitimate phone system to leave voice mails. It isn't fancy, but it does its job.

Distinct: Distinct means you take competitive to a higher level. You offer things at longer hours, offer more access, or provide additional value. For example:

- You offer an online chat on your web site to communicate with clients and prospects.
- You commit to visiting your clients on a quarterly basis with an agenda and plan of action.
- You offer "just in time" certificates and binders that go out within 15 minutes.
- You offer free webinars on your web site as resources.

Breakthrough: Breakthrough means you are the only one in your market doing this OR you are unique because you have skills that others can't match. The legendary rock and roll front man for The Grateful Dead, Jerry Garcia once quipped, *"It's one thing to be the best. It's even better to be the only one."* Breakthrough usually means it something only you can do. For example:

- You've created a template or matrix to assist homeowners in cataloging and storing important data about their property. You created it and it's unlike anything else they will find.
- You offer 24/7 personal access to clients through a private mobile phone.
- You offer a unique series of articles, resources, and videos done by you to help your clients save money and improve their protection.
- You offer a personal mobile app for clients to access you or important information.
- You provide unique complimentary services outside the scope of placing business.

You can't be distinct and breakthrough in everything, nor should you try to be. Here is an easy-to-comprehend template to use as a guide.

Competitive: Expertise; business office hours; free mailings and newsletters; turnaround time for simple requests; return standards for calls and emails; and community involvement.

Distinct: Personal access to you; web site access and controls; frequency of visits; hospitality to visitors to your office; and being an intermediary with other insurance services (e.g. claims, service call centers, underwriters and interviewers).

Breakthrough: Intellectual property you create; unique services only you can offer; and private admittance to connect with you.

You may have noticed that I put **expertise** in competitive. Some of you may question this, so hear me out. Being expert makes you competitive with your rivals. Anyone can learn insurance. Being 10 times smarter doesn't make the client 10 times better. As a matter of fact, I've seen agents that were overly discerning often talk their way out of business, not into it. They usually need jobs as risk managers or service specialists. Your clients don't need you to know everything all the time. They need you to be fully capable and able to find out answers quickly when it's necessary. Your availability and skill in responsiveness, availability, patience, empathy, resources, uniqueness, and insight are what they want.

I am a director on the school board of education in my city. When I first came on the board, I found that the flood of information being hurled at me was overwhelming. To make matters worse, much of it was just data-driven minutia that didn't impact any decision I might need to make (a commonplace occurrence with many in academia). It bordered on exasperating at times. I learned that the primary reason for this was that administrators were getting pressure from some colleagues who were data driven themselves, to provide very quantitative information. I finally said to them, "Tell me what I need to know, not everything you know." This was an astonishing yet welcome statement for them. Turns out I wasn't the only one that wanted my information this way. Even my "data" colleagues did. Why would you provide more than what was needed to make a decision to someone who is not expert in the field? Insurance agents do this far too often! My recommendation to you if you are is…STOP!

The bottom line is that you must choose what it is that makes your agency distinct and breakthrough. That is where you put your emphasis on promotion and recognition. This is part of your value proposition. Which by chance is NEXT…

Creating a value proposition

Why is someone better off working with you? How have you improved their condition? I'm not interested in hearing about great customer service and how much you care about your clients. Those are givens and overused statements in your profession. In an industry where the products are vastly similar and the transaction process simple to start, you have to create an image of difference that makes your client say, "I would never leave, Sally," and intrigue your prospects enough to give you a shot at their business.

I buy my cars from one guy in town. Kevin is a salesman in what would be considered an "upscale" used car dealership. The dealership has all the look and feel of a new car place, has high quality vehicles in its lot, and all the sales professionals act like professionals. Kevin is one of these guys and our family will only consider buying from him. In another industry that appears to be highly competitive and commoditized, he has provided us an image of difference that keeps us from even considering someone else. Here are a few examples:

- He has never tried to "sell" us. Each purchase has been on our terms and he has been patient in the process. He is THE expert and we trust his judgement.

- Every time I come into the shop to have my car worked on, he comes over and greets me. He knows I'm not in the buying phase, but he takes time out to come over and chat. This may seem minor, but it's part of that relationship we always talk about.
- He consistently mails hard copy newsletters mailed to us with new and used vehicles they currently have in stock.
- He always asks about our kids and knows their names.
- When my daughter was searching for a car while living across the country, Kevin offered and did pull Vehicle Identification Numbers (VIN) to assist her in making the right purchase.

Kevin has over the years demonstrated he is more than just a guy that has the ability to sell us a car. He has created value for us at every step of our relationship, whether or not we are purchasing a car.

What's your value proposition? Other than selling a life insurance, car insurance, business insurance, or any other type of policy – what value do you bring to your clients?

If I were still an agent today, I would focus on the one thing that I believe is the common denominator for the majority of preferred insurance buyers today. That is the value of protecting a ***lifestyle***. In the end, all insurances protect the ability to, at the very minimum, keep one's lifestyle intact. At I write this book, I'm 48 years old. When I'm 68 years old, I want to have a richer lifestyle. However there are some things out of my control. That being said, I am fiercely guarding the lifestyle I have today to assure that I will at least have that. The same is true for 78, 88, and 98, if I get there. Wouldn't you admit the same thing for yourself?

So how does one fiercely guard one's lifestyle? You're an expert in managing risk, so you know the answer to that question:

1. You determine your exposures and potential hazards and perils
2. You make changes that you can to improve your odds
3. You transfer your risk for catastrophic loss that you can't afford to pay yourself
4. You live your life with a peace of mind.

Let's examine a couple of examples of this principle…

Hazard/Peril	Changing Odds	Risk Transfer
Loss of income/death	Exercise, diet, life balance	Life insurance to cover current and future expenses
Loss of home/fire	Sprinkler system, good wiring, fire extinguishers	Homeowner's insurance
Loss of life's work and equity/business property and casualty	Crisis planning and prevention, protective systems, hiring practices	Business insurance
Loss of estate/elderly and aging issues	Diet, exercise, medications	Long-term care insurance

Bottom line – Your value proposition is all about how you can improve and protect your client's lifestyle through risk transfer. The more ways outside of placing coverage that you can offer them, the more valuable and indispensible a business partner you become. Here are ***Dan's 9 Ways to add immeasurable value*** to your clients to make yourself competition-proof:

1. **Talk to them when things are good.** All too often, the only time people hear from insurance agents is when there has been a claim, a cancellation, a non-renewal, or some other negative issue. Give them a call just to see how they are doing.

2. **Talk to them about things other than insurance.** Send them tips on their favorite hobbies. Learn about their kids and the colleges they are going to. Invite them to a service club or charity organization. Help them see you as more than just a person who sells and talks insurance.

3. **Call them with important information about insurance.** If there has been an earthquake somewhere, call and discuss the merits of that coverage to them. Invite them to have a discussion about it. If there is a law change that affects their decision-making on their life insurance, call and apprise them of what the effects are. Don't leave it solely to your insurance carrier to do all the legwork. Be proactive.

4. **Send them regular correspondence.** It might be electronic or hard copy newsletters or other mailings. Fill these with valuable information on how to save money, improve protection, keep their car running longer, etc. Keep "dripping" yourself into their consciousness, and make sure it's valuable.

5. **Insure all their accounts.** Mono-line selling is a "lose-lose" proposition. It's bad for you (costs more to service) and bad for them (potential gaps in coverage). Be bold enough to educate people on why having all their insurance with one agent is to their advantage. It's not about the money and commissions. It's about assuring that there will be no disparity in protection and that they only have one place they need to call.

6. **Thank them…often.** Thank them at renewals, when they call, and intermittently. No need to be obsequious; however it is wise to express your gratitude for their business. People need to hear it more than the one time they purchased the policy! The more you thank them, the greater the likelihood of them feeling awkward about checking out your competition.

> *Note*: A value proposition is NOT an elevator speech. Elevator speeches might work if you're selling an elevator. Value propositions work if you're selling insurance.

Your value proposition pops up when someone at a cocktail party, business social, or airplane seat next to you asks you what you do for a living. The common answer is *"I sell insurance."* The next sound you hear is the sudden whoosh of the person's head turning away to avoid any further communications. Your value proposition should answer these questions, in this order – Whom do you help? What are you protecting or avoiding? What is the positive result? In the end, your value proposition may sound something like one of these…

"I help families to protect their lifestyle regardless of what life throws at them."

"I help business owners protect their years of blood, sweat, and tears to assure they will be able to maximize their years of investment."

"I help individuals assure that no matter what calamity befalls them, they will always have an income to support themselves."

"I assure that your parent's estate and your inheritance won't be decimated in the event of a move to a nursing home or skilled facility."

"I help you make decisions now, so they won't need to be made in the midst of a crisis later."

The beautiful thing is that our industry is a very dignified one. We protect people's lives, fortunes, and dreams. We help them avoid cataclysms and live life with peace of mind. Somehow our value proposition has over the years become solely about saving money and who has the goofiest commercial. Centuries ago, the Chinese realized that doing business without protection was foolhardy. That has turned into a business that now not only protects business, but protects people and their lifestyles too.

Accessibility and communications

The biggest complaint I hear from insurance buyers is that they don't ever hear from their agent, except at renewal when they want money. I also incorporate the complaints of indifference in returning calls. Agents need to understand this "new normal" factoid – in today's instant messaging kind of world, accessibility is no longer a benefit, it's a given. Returning calls to clients and prospects should be the highest priority. Why this isn't happening is actually pretty simple to sum up in one of four reasons:

1. **Laziness** – If you're lazy, you'd better snap out of it. This is not the avocation for the uninspired and unmotivated. Everyone can be replaced and people that are simply lazy about callbacks generally end up unemployed.
2. **Poor time management** – Take a class or get coaching. There might be just less than a gazillion books on time management available to you. Get a referral to someone good, buy the book, and learn from it. Find a coach to help you prioritize. This is too important for your career.
3. **Disorganization** – I know this sounds simple, but get organized. This was (and sometimes still is) one of my biggest areas of weakness. Many agents who are rock stars in sales have the personality traits to be, let's say, brutally unorganized. The best things to do are admit it, get help, and continually work at staying on top of things. Technology gives us outstanding tools for process and structure when it comes to contact management. Find one that works for you and use it.
4. **Scared to call back** – Why are you scared? Did you mess something up? Did you accidentally offend someone? Did they change their mind and get buyer's remorse? Whatever it is, not calling back quickly will only make it worse. More often than not, the thing you were scared about wasn't a problem at all. They might want to actually give you a referral!

None of these are acceptable to someone in the professional services business. If you are the sales manager, you must give guidance to your agency's standards and make sure your agents are accountable to that. In an age of smart phones, text messaging, social media, and other new and evolving communication devices, not being accessible and able to communicate should never be a delivery problem. It's always a personal problem!

When I started my consulting practice, I adopted a response standard that was set by my mentor, Scott Simmonds. Scott used the same timeline as his mentor, and my future mentor, Alan Weiss, of 90 minutes for a phone call and 24 hours for email. This was in 2005. I still keep the same time standard when I get a voice mail, yet have adjusted others. I now include text like a voice mail, and email as same day. In 2005 I wasn't carrying around an iPhone that gave me instantaneous email. I had to wait to get back to the office. That is no longer true, so returning an email should rarely take more than a few hours if only to at least acknowledge that you received it. My clients are literally dumbstruck that I set these standards, but are happy. They don't get those commitments from other business partners.

I've seen hundreds of insurance proposals and summaries since I left the agency world. In almost all cases, agents give exhaustive information about every member of their team, including direct phone lines, emails, mobile numbers, and ICE numbers (In Case of Emergency). They might even plaster everyone's pictures next to their names just for good measure. They encourage new clients to call or write them any time. But nowhere have I ever seen where they've promised to call back in a specific amount of time. Agents will say things like, "We will call you right back." What does that mean? Put in paper that you will call back in less than 90 minutes. Commit to responding to email in less than one hour. Stop leaving voice mails with the maddening phrase, "I will call you back at my earliest convenience." Well, if you're on vacation to Bora Bora, that might be awhile.

Here are my keys to being truly accessible to your clients and gaining great trust and loyalty from them…

- **Be specific and say it or write it.** You will respond within 3 hours. The "next day" just doesn't cut it unless it's 4:15. In today's email and text crazy world, if you get a call as an insurance agent, it's probably pretty important! Make your clients a priority and call them back promptly.
- **Utilize technology.** Find out which clients like to use text messaging and then use it. If they prefer email, return their correspondence from your smart phone or notebook.
- **Acknowledge receipt.** You may not have the answer they are looking for. Don't wait until you get it. Send a quick response confirming receipt of

their request and let them know you're working on it. Then tell them when you're going to call them back.

- **When they've contacted you, shut up and listen.** They have some need. Don't engage in small talk on these calls. Ask them how you can help and then let them go.
- **Be open about what your response times are** and make a promise that you will keep it. If you're out on vacation, delegate it and advise your clients. Just because you're gone doesn't mean they won't need to talk to someone.
- **Delegate.** Educate your clients on what they should be calling you about, what they should be calling your assistant about, and what they should be calling the company service center about. I guarantee you, with a little teaching; you will greatly reduce the number of calls you get. Stand firm on this. It's in your client's best interest, and it helps your management of calls.

Bottom line is that you are being held to a higher standard when it comes to accessibility and communications. This is no longer a benefit, but a given (when I say it twice, that means it's *really* important). If you are falling short on this, take the necessary steps to get better. Your clients will love you for it.

Personal branding

Insurance buyers of all types don't buy insurance from companies. They buy them from people. Some person made enough of an impression on them to persuade the purchase. You have to be able to build your own personal brand to assure that the person top of mind when it comes to insurance in your area of expertise is YOU!

> I understand people buy online today, especially when it comes to personal lines and life insurance. If they called a toll free number and talked to a real human being, that was the person of influence. If they bought it themselves, they are badly underinsured and need your help, so find them!

Your agency or your company invest a whole bunch of money to market and brand themselves. You don't have that kind of coin, but you don't need it. You can simply follow my 3 Simple Rules for Better Branding for Insurance Pros…

1. **Use your name early and often.** Even if you work for an agency, your name is top of mind for your prospect when they are ready to look at insurance. The more you brand your name, the more they will think of you. Brand your name in your email signature, your business cards, your intellectual property, your voice mail, and your marketing and advertising. Don't rely on the name of your agency, unless they are the same! Rely on people remembering your name.
2. **Be active in the right business groups.** Even if your insurance is aimed at individuals, people in the business community often make the best personal clients. Join and be active in chambers of commerce, Rotary Clubs, other civic groups like Lions and Kiwanis, trade groups and associations, and potentially even networking groups. The last one is a group to be wary of. Make sure their process lines up with you and your target market. Many networking groups are all about referral business that is forced and contrived. Don't waste your time there. Find peer business partners that you can work with.
3. **Be active in your community.** You have to be sincere in your desire to improve aspects of your community, so only become involved in charity work that you have a passion for. Your work will not only benefit those less fortunate, but will also show that you are part of a larger community and that always helps in brand appeal.

The sales manager: Growing and developing in a complex world

Sales managers notoriously are born from very successful producers who are "promoted." This invariably turns out to be a terrible decision. Here is why...

1. **Producers are wired to sell.** The most successful ones are expressive, gregarious, and influential. They are also very high energy, tend to lack discipline, need oversight, and are not detail-oriented.
2. **Managers manage other people.** I know that doesn't come as a startling revelation to all of you, but so many agency owners seem to forget that when hiring a sales manager. To manage others, you need to have skills such as being detail-oriented, on task, good at meeting mileposts, time management savvy, and a teacher.

3. **Sales people want to keep selling.** They maximize their talent and make more money that way. Managers want to make others better because when those people succeed, they make more money.

Here is an example.

Tiger Woods may be the greatest golfer of all time. In an era where the game is more global and more widely competed than ever, his domination in a 10-year period is remarkable. Tiger Woods is the equivalent of a rock star producer. This producer has the steak and the sizzle. They have the experience and the unbounded self-confidence that they can win every time. In sports vernacular, they "got game."

Tiger Woods has a manager. I'm not talking about his swing coach, putting coach, or mental coach. These people are all important, but they work on the methodology of the game. Tiger's manager is his agent and business advisor. The manager works on his endorsements, his contracts, and his brand. He's there when Tiger needs to vent, to get advice, and to take the next steps. I don't know this for a fact, but my guess is that his manager might have trouble winning his club championship, much less be anywhere near a professional golfer. His skill is in managing and guiding Tiger Woods to be the best he can be and turn that skill into reward.

As an agency owner, you need to clearly understand this. If your agency is set up to have several producers and a manager, you must put the right pieces of the puzzle in the right places. That means properly hiring a sales manager. If you promote a rock star producer, your results are a bad double whammy. You remove a top producer so that their production is severely hampered, and you have a manager who doesn't know how to manage and your sales from others suffer.

Here is how you deal with getting the right person in the position of sales manager:

1. You promote or hire a person who has a managerial skill set first. Yes, this person should have some experience selling, but they shouldn't have been the "rainmaker." Those guys and gals need to keep selling. This person must be adept at managing people.

2. You pay them a base salary with incentives based on the performance of their team. They need to believe they are best served when the team is successful. Producers believe they are best served when they are in control of their own fortune.

3. You offer whatever outside managerial training you can find. My guess is there are plenty of educational opportunities between company carriers, trade associations, and other services.

4. They will report directly to you. You will offer guidance, support, and help.
5. You remove restrictions from their sales production. While it's fine that they are still able to do some selling, if you put high expectations for both producing and managing, you will end up with a burned out and bitter employee.

Sales managers should be long on patience, education, discipline, and metrics. They should have enough success to be able to have credibility, yet not to the point that they resent coaching and mentoring others. Just because a person can sell, doesn't mean they can manage people.

For all you sports nuts out there, do a quick mental check. When you consider the Big 4 in professional sports – football, baseball, basketball, and hockey – what percentage of great coaches were also great players? Not many. My guess is it's by far the exception, not the norm. The reason is that great athletes are wired differently. They were great on the field or court, and those traits don't transfer over to managing others. They were experts in managing themselves. They are rarely expert in motivating and sometimes babysitting others.

If you own a small agency and you have to wear many hats (owner, producer, and sales manager), then this becomes a challenge. I know I have personally coached several agency owners of small agencies where their biggest hurdle was juggling employee management (sales and support) and their own production. If you are forced to be the sales manager, then take these few steps to help you maximize your own talent and that of your team:

- **Get over yourself.** You may have sold gobs of insurance in your day, but your methods, practices, or tactics may not match the times or the talents of your sales force. There are many and new ways to skin that proverbial cat. You are there to guide and hold accountable, not to be cantankerous and boorish.
- **Get training.** Find some of those educational opportunities to sharpen managerial skills. Hire a coach or mentor to guide you and be a source of support as you learn. This requires humility and vulnerability, yet in actuality requires the highest level of self-confidence.

- **Make specific and regular time on your calendar to meet with your producers both individually and collectively.** That means these meetings are sacrosanct. Be attentive and in the moment with your team to help them. Keep agendas and accountability at the forefront of your discussions. Do more listening than talking.
- **Learn how to create and monitor metrics.** It's one thing to know what metrics are; it's another thing to know what to do with them! You must hold them accountable, and the only way you do that is by ensuring they have something worth being accountable for.
- **Reduce your own production time.** Focus on marketing your agency. If you do a good job as a sales manager, then the fruits of your labor will come through your team. The result is a team that is building confidence and control, and an owner (you) that is reaping the rewards. This behavior is not as easy as it sounds and requires focus and discipline.

Bottom line – don't make the mistake that so many agency principals make. Don't simply make someone a sales manager because they are superlative in sales. Create roles and responsibilities based on skill and personality, and you will have a better sales manager and a better sales team.

The sales manager bonus section: How do you measure up?

Mike Hall is the President and CEO of Hall & Company in Poulsbo, Washington. Hall & Company is a national broker that specializes in professional liability for architects and engineers, professional liability for insurance agents, and insurance protection for attorneys. They have a staff of about 50 people, with an emphasis on telemarketing, direct sales, and client service. Mr. Hall is a client of mine and one of the things I'm most impressed with is the sheer intensity he places on metrics and measuring output for producers and staff. And, it might not be what you expect.

I spent a morning over coffee with Mike to discuss what this increased emphasis on collecting data has meant to the company in both revenue increase and intangible value. Mike is a straight shooter with a quick wit, and someone willing to share his experiences. While my interview had a set series of questions, when you "interview" Mike, you end up in more of a conversation. Here are the highlights...

Question – *Your background is engineering and management. This is different from most insurance agency owners' and executives' backgrounds. How do you think this expertise has helped you create a model of metrics for your company?*

Answer – "Math is easy for me. Looking at data is basically second nature. I think the management background is more important than the math. In management, the concept is that if you want to be good at something, you have to measure it. That's what we do here."

Dan's 2 cents – *While I fully admit that most insurance company carrier executives come from a management background and are as enthusiastic about metrics and measurements as Mike is, the average agency owner or executive isn't. They usually surfaced as the big boss in one of three ways.*

First, they were once rock star producers. This gave them the credibility, influence, and resources to be able to get to the position they have.

Second, many come in to the captive agencies with some sort of background in sales, marketing, or entrepreneurship. They find being an owner of a nationally recognized company like State Farm, Farmers, Allstate, or American Family will give them the rewards of being their own boss and doing what they like as part of a larger organization.

Third, many of you out there are second and third generation owners. You grew up in the business, at one time swore you'd never enter it, and then ultimately succumbed when you saw what kind of lifestyle and personal satisfaction it could provide you.

Bottom line – you probably came into this business as a sales specialist. Your emphasis was on making contacts and closing deals. Setting up measurements and metrics for success wasn't necessarily high on your list of priorities.

Question – *What caused the change to this relatively new system of assessing metrics that you're using?*

Answer – "I found that we were good at indirect marketing, but not so good at direct marketing. When I had a chance to see how Lockton (an insurance and risk management company out of Kansas City) operated, I thought, 'We have a lot to learn.' I came back knowing that we needed to make changes."

***Dan's 2 cents:** What Mike explained was that Lockton was terrific at a more proactive model of sales. While Hall & Company was excellent once the application came in, Lockton was fastidious about getting apps to come in. Mike broke down the sales cycle into three areas – Get the x-date; Get the application; Close the Deal. The beginning numbers were low at the start in the x-date column. However over the years that has improved. The beauty of how he tracks his producers is that he can look at all three areas and determine where they are strong, and where they might need improvement. For example, if they are getting a lot of x-dates but not converting them into applications, that area needs to be examined. Without the data to back it up, you're just making guesses.*

My conjecture is that many of you are shooting from the hip. You have no idea how many contacts your producers are making, how many are turning into legitimate prospects, how many of those are turning into applications to quote, and finally how many are converted into new business. I guarantee that if I called Mike up this afternoon and asked him those numbers, he could get them in five minutes. What about you?

Question – *Was this process easy to implement or were there challenges with your team?*

Answer – "Resistance is inherent with change. The key to measurement is transparency. I want my people to look at the data themselves and figure out how to respond to it. I was looking for their interpretations and response. My desire was to improve the company. That wasn't always the desire of everyone else. When the data and results are transparent, you have no place to hide. Over the past several years, we have changed the culture and encourage debates and the results are that people now want transparency. An example is that our effectiveness of gaining x-dates has gone from 25% to 35% in a short time. That's a result of overcoming the resistance by either converting those people or having them move on. In the end, it's about creating a culture."

***Dan's 2 cents** – When I coached high school basketball, as a team we would always watch game film to see how we did. I used to tell my players, "Video never lies." If you missed blocking out a player, it was there for all your teammates to see. Conversely, if you set a strong screen, you were given your due praise and credit.*

For Hall & Company, the metrics don't lie. If you aren't being successful because you didn't work the plan, it will be clear to everyone. There is no place to hide. If you are doing your job, you can prove it and the results will be there. Even if you're struggling in an area, that will be indicated by those results and can be something to be analyzed and righted. One of Mike's favorite phrases is that people can self-select to be terminated. One way to do this is to not adhere to this transparency. Mike's biggest takeaway from this is that by using metrics and measurement of data that are transparent, you actually improve and define your culture.

How transparent is your agency? Does everyone really know how the team is performing? Do you really know?

Question – *Do you measure performance of non-producers? If so, how?*

Answer – "Yes. We measure our customer service representatives (CSRs) to assess workload and determine if we have the right balance. We apply weighted algorithms to assess the workload and then reallocate as needed to keep that balance."

Dan's 2 cents – *One of the areas of angst for many agencies (both small and large) is how to effectively manage the service team. What happens in too many cases is that workloads get wonky and CSRs become disproportionately utilized. At Hall & Company, they use a bevy of factors, which they weigh separately based on how it impacts workload – size, complexity, number of certificates required, number of accounts, etc. One of the things that Mike discovered was that all too often, the person doing the least was the one doing the most complaining. When a reallocation was done, there would be a "sense of relief" for those producing and working effectively, while the others would feel the "cold chill" of reality set in.*

It can be hard and time consuming to measure the effectiveness of your staff. Heck, you might only have a staff of two people as compared to the dozens that Hall & Company have. Regardless, once those polices are written, you will be evaluated by your clientele as to how responsive and efficient your staff is. When you start getting complaints that normally means it's worse than you think. Being proactive in this area is worth your attention.

Question – *What did I miss asking you? What more would you like to share?*

Answers – "There has to be a willingness to make hard decisions *after* you get all the data. Analysis Paralysis can too easily occur and nothing happens. You will get things done quicker and see improvements faster when you make those hard decisions that the data shows you."

"It's better to make long-term decisions on employment based on facts, rather than on 'feel.'

"There is a cost of technology and time that needs to be considered. We choose to go on an incremental model. Many people (even us) can't afford all of the systems out there. You have to decide what you most need and what technology to implement based on your operation"

"This approach is about supporting ***culture***. We want people that are drawn to high work effort. There are a lot of smart people out there that don't work. We are looking for smart and humble. That building block fits with measuring because it gets people in and functioning quickly. I think that we can get new people to a five-year mark of efficiency within two years based on our system. We beat the "Prima Donna" out of them by starting at the bottom and have them do everything from the bottom up. Then they appreciate the support we provide them later because they know how much work it is."

Dan's 2 cents – *Mike indicates that the company has grown by 20% in a time when many agencies are struggling to stay flat. He believes it's the commitment to tracking and measuring that has developed a culture of excellence in building a team that is running on all cylinders. While there are always challenges, the more transparency there is, the right people for his team will gravitate toward it. The results have been undeniable.*

My questions for you are these:

1. *How can you implement even a slice of this section into your agency?*
2. *What did you walk away with that most resonated?*

If I were in your shoes, I would find a way to measure what you find most valuable to you. Commit to it and start creating a culture of transparency and accountability. The people that don't "buy in" will effectively self-select themselves out of a job. The good news is that those who do dedicate themselves to improvement and are willing to be ingenuous about it will blossom. And so will your culture, your clients, and your revenues.

Chapter 4

Hi Tech, Hello Touch

How you reach people through, around, and despite the web

In November of 2010, I had a conversation with a colleague of mine at a summit with my professional consulting community. Earlier that year, she had spoken at a large executive conference in Bogota, Colombia. I was intrigued because Bogota is where my mother was born and grew up; it was where I had many family members; and it's also a place that I had not visited in 40 years. I wanted to learn how she did it, and if she would offer me an introduction to her contact.

Simma was very kind and provided me with the organization's name and her contact, along with his contact information. Personal referrals are the platinum standard for acquiring business, even if that business is public speaking. When I returned from the summit, I immediately fired off an email introducing myself and inquiring about opportunities for the coming year to speak at one of their events. Simma had warned me that her contact was a bit slow to respond to emails, so I should be persistent.

After sending the message, I decided to check them out a little bit more. In addition to looking at the organization's web site, I went on their Facebook page to see what they offered there. In 2010, not all organizations had a Facebook presence, but America Empresarial did. Something in my head said, "Dan, why don't you send them a message through their Facebook page? It might speed up the process." It turned out to be the decisive move in this relationship.

I copied and pasted my email message into the Facebook Instant Messaging portal and hit "send." I didn't have to wait more than 10 minutes for a response. It turned out that Simma's contact no longer worked for America Empresarial. As my email didn't bounce back, I might still be waiting until today to get a response, thinking that this guy was *really* hard to contact! The person in charge of social media correspondence quickly introduced me to the new person, who was much more responsive. The end result is that we sealed the deal in two days for me to go to Bogota to speak several months later. I was able to launch a more global marketing front and visit my relatives all through the wonders of social media. Had it not been for Facebook, I would not have made this connection and new business.

Social Media is here to stay. What it looks like in the next 5, 10, or 15 years is uncertain. What is certain is that it will change and look completely different than it does today. Heck, by the time I'm done writing this book, getting it printed, and finally distributed, to the point you are now reading it, parts of this monolith of the technological world may be altogether different. The message to you in this chapter, however, is much more simple. In order to be successful in the insurance business, you must embrace technology, make it your friend, give it a comfortable seat, and make sure you stay on the cutting edge of that friendship. Otherwise, it will get bored with you and leave.

Consider this chapter your guide to becoming a BFF (Best Friend Forever for those of you without teenage children) with social media. We will discuss how to stay on the cutting edge, and how to maximize your ability to acquire and keep clients.

Defining social media

Lets first do a little *defining* before we dig into how to use social media correctly. Unless you've been living under a rock for the past five years, you have heard of, used personally, and understand the term "social media." What I want to quickly accomplish with you here is to define social media for you as a *business tool*, and highlight the platforms you should concentrate on. As of today, I recommend the four most popular social media platforms for business use – Facebook, Twitter, YouTube, and LinkedIn. By the time you're reading this, it may have changed and expanded. That's my point about technology; you need to be savvy enough to stay up with the curve, not necessarily ahead of it. If you fall behind, you may just leave business in the wake.

Facebook

You need to have a business page presence on Facebook. Facebook's reach and breadth has soared just in the past two years. To say that Facebook is widely read and utilized globally is like acknowledging that mustard is yellow. People perform searches on Facebook almost as much as they do on search engines. You must have an existence with a specific business page. This does NOT mean a personal page dressed up to include your business. They need to be separate because the messages and audiences are different. And, sending mixed messages can create doom and gloom in your business arena.

Funny...one of my daughters has cut back on Facebook significantly. Why? In her words, "Adults have ruined it." Let's just say Facebook isn't just for kids anymore!

Twitter

Twitter is the very best option you have to quickly and pithily get value out to the world. Being subject to under 140 characters forces you to be brief yet powerful. Depending on your market, Twitter just might be THE resource that gets the most action. Technology has always been about getting smaller and Twitter has embraced that in the forms of limiting characters. It's completely changed conversation by being minimalist. We as insurance professionals can learn from it. Our prospects want to hear more with less. Consider this your opportunity to give it to them.

YouTube

Video is the name of the game in the 21st century. As technology advances, we as a society become more "visual." YouTube (now owned by Google) has changed the world on how we can disseminate business information. Yes, there are now competitors. However, with the Google brand behind it, YouTube will continue to be the leader in the field.

YouTube offers you the opportunity to run your own television channel for free. You should take advantage of that. You can promote upcoming events, hold an event, send out valuable information, create a video newsletter, or share a recent presentation. You can even become your own TED network! Not taking advantage of the power of video that comes at no cost is being foolish.

LinkedIn

If Facebook is the cocktail party and Twitter is the "kegger," then LinkedIn is the office water cooler. You simply must create a presence on LinkedIn because it's another source of credibility. Linked In allows you to build your profile to be viewed by others who are searching for something. If they found you, undoubtedly it's insurance! Fill your profile with intellectual property, videos, testimonials, referrals, industry awards and certifications, etc. It's nearly as good as a web site for individuals and may be more likely to be found.

LinkedIn is also a terrific place to research your prospects, especially if you're in the business market. Its search engine will let you "stalk" individuals, companies, and groups. It's now easier than ever to learn about someone you have made an appointment with. Power is knowledge, so learn how to harness the power for your good.

What's your message?

Social media is the foremost way to toot your own horn. It's free, it's global, it's viral, and it's relatively easy to learn. It offers you a tremendous opportunity for high "touch" with your prospects and clients. Unfortunately, most insurance agents either don't use it, or use it poorly. Like anything else, there is a process. What I hear most often from insurance agents is, "I don't know what to say." My response is, "What do you say when you're with them face to face?" The truth is that you now have a broader audience and you control how your information is heard. This sub-section will discuss the "what" about your message.

In the last chapter, we discussed *value proposition*. Your value proposition is your "message." Stop filling your social media with gibberish about you. Start promoting how you can help improve the condition of your client.

Case Study

Let's say you're a personal lines insurance agent. Your products include auto, home, umbrella, life, and long-term care. You have some options about what you can talk about, yet the most important are these four classifications - ***price, coverage, financial sustainability, and them***. Let's use this case study to see how it's done.

Note – if you sell commercial insurance, the case study still works. The classifications basically remain the same, with the emphasis on business continuation. Don't skip this part of you're not a personal lines agent. You still will receive ideas on the "what" of maximizing your message on social media.

Price - Now by simply watching television commercials, you might think that price is the best option. That's what 90% of the ads believe people want to hear. The only reason they do is because we've smashed it down their throats! In reality, most people buy insurance to *protect their lifestyle*. Think about yourself. Say you're in your mid-40s, have a family, a nice home (with a mortgage), a couple of cars, and maybe a recreational vehicle of some sort. In 25 years, you expect that your lifestyle will not have gone down, but up. At the very least, you want to assure that it stays the same. What things happen that alter lifestyles? How about the death of a wage earner, a house fire, theft of property, a terrible accident that disables a member of the family, or a loss of job? You might add many more ideas. Transferring that risk through insurance can mitigate the vast majority of them. Too many of your clients have been trained to think of insurance as a necessary evil. You need to help people see that the insurance premium is simply a function of insuring a lifestyle. That message often takes away price resistance because lifestyle is something that we deem as highly valuable. You can send this message that buying insurance solely on price is dangerous because you place your lifestyle at stake.

Coverage – This term has many meanings. The only significance that your client or prospect cares about is "protection." You have the opportunity here to educate your audience. They are constantly bombarded with goofy commercials about insurance. While these commercials are clever and probably get the desired result (phone calls), they don't provide real value. You have that chance through social media.

What can you promote as a personal lines agent? You can send out information on the following topics:

- Scheduled jewelry and other items
- Auto Physical Damage issues
- Business use in a personal residence
- Protection for property and autos that your child has at college
- Liability related to dogs and other pets
- Host liquor liability from parties at the home
- Typical exclusions

The list goes on, and I know that if you spend 15 minutes brainstorming, you could add dozens. My point is that you can add the tremendous value to your target market that is not propagated in television ads.

Financial Sustainability – This is the section that most applies to lifestyle protection. While much of insurance buying is focused on the bad things that might happen, attention should be paid to the good things that happen in the future. People want to be no worse off in the future than they are right now. You need to be talking about that. Here are some examples of topics...

- Life insurance to protect lifestyle of family in the event of a death
- Disability insurance to protect lifestyle in the event of an income earner being unable to work
- Personal Liability to protect the investments and savings in the event of a catastrophic lawsuit
- Auto insurance (not as a necessity) as a means to ensure you have transportation in the event of an accident
- Long-term care protection for your life savings in the event of needing to enter a skilled nursing facility.

This protection of assets and ultimately lifestyle gets overlooked with the constant clamor of saving money now. You have the chance to educate people on true "insurance," and in a meaningful way for them.

Them – People concern themselves with that old adage of "what's in it for me," or WIIFM. That's what advertisers focus on. These ad executives understand the principle that logic makes people think, emotion makes people act. "Emotion" is all about values, priorities, self-esteem, self-worth, the "cool" factor, and much more. Insurance ads are targeted at the WIIFM when it comes to saving money so you can spend it on other fun things (priority), going with a company endorsed by a celebrity (cool factor), and just plain humor as bait to call or visit the web site. Through social media, you have a platform to talk about other emotions, such as...

- Peace of mind
- Simplicity
- Loss of use
- Reduction of fear

The bottom line is that you are better than TV ads, and can have more impact. You actually know what's better for them. You're the expert, not a gecko, girl in a white jump suit, or 24/7 call center. As a professional agent, you have the expertise and knowledge. It's time you shared it!

The How – So how do you do this? Learn to write and speak powerfully and with conviction and influence. You should be well down that path if you're a successful agent already. Now you just need to take that intellectual capital (your "smarts") and manifest it in intellectual property (articles, published work, speaking). That means blog posts, business columns, podcasts, webinars, teleconferences, videos, etc. All this work can be shared on social media on the platforms I mentioned earlier – Facebook, Twitter, YouTube, and LinkedIn. This does take a commitment as part of your marketing plan. You need to be aware that this by itself doesn't come with instant gratification but like all effective long-term marketing, it acts as a strong enhancement that keeps your name visible in your community, however big that community needs to be.

Web site "cred"

"Cred" is slang for credibility. You probably knew that, but just in case, there it is! As an insurance agency or company, your web site serves only to provide that – credibility. Unfortunately, about 85% of boutique insurance agency web sites are terrible. They are obsolete, incomplete, poorly written, and not engaging to the visitor. Slang for that is "boring!" These agents probably still think that spending money on yellow page ads is the best investment in their marketing money.

Web sites are the primary way that buyers will check you out. Many of you are starting to get the picture as I have seen in my work a sharp increase in web site efficacy (that translates to about 10% improvement). This section is meant to help all of you enhance your web site so it becomes a force for good, not decrepitude.

What your web site should include – Your web site is the place people go to learn about you, discover why they should do business with you, and make sure you know what you're talking about.

Here is a short list of what your site needs to include. Understand that you can do more; this is a baseline. Also remember that simplicity always rules the day. Steve Jobs made that perfectly clear at Apple, and it catapulted them to the front in technology, digital music, and entertainment. Make sure your web site includes all of these; yet make it user friendly and simple for your visitor…

- **Videos** – include video testimonials from happy clients, brief video excerpts that provide value and guidance, and maybe even a brief video message from the agency owner.
- **Testimonials** – Written testimonials should be ubiquitous – on every page. Have them scroll through in places where your visitor will see them. Nothing is as valuable to someone checking out your business as a strong testimonial from a peer.
- **Resource Center** – This can include articles, podcasts, videos, or other information where people can learn about insurance and the issues that affect them.
- **Easy access to staff** – A visitor should be able to *quickly* find an agent or support staff to contact them. They should be able to view a photo of the person and with one click either email or call them. Instant messaging is becoming an even bigger deal today.

I recently needed to contact Capital One as I thought I had lost my Visa card from them (turns out it was buried under a book on my desk – oh well). I found a button that enabled me to chat instantly with a representative. The time between my clicking it and "James" responding was all of about one second. We had a five-minute "conversation" before I uncovered my card and no longer needed his services. Regardless, "James" was easy to access, helpful, polite, and made the experience pleasant. Can your agency find a way to do that?

- **Client Services** – Once they are your client, they should have a place on your site to gain access to documents like certificates of insurance, auto identification cards, applications, templates, or anything else that they might be able to use and get on their own quickly.
- **Typical Client Results** – This section should identify what new clients can expect from working with you. This should be filled with value statements. Do you offer annual client reviews to ensure there are never any gaps in coverage? Do you guarantee a response time to voice mails and emails to improve communications and timeliness? Do you provide cutting edge web site technology to save them time? Fill one page with typical client results, and make sure they always answer the questions – *"So what? Who Cares? What's in it for me?"*

- **Specialty Programs** – If you have a program or programs that you specialize in, this should be highlighted. This might be especially true in commercial lines or benefits.
- **Photos** – Just like videos, images influence and impact your reader. Show photos of staff, of your agents working with clients, and being in the field. Be creative with clip art and process visuals. DO NOT get goofy with highly technical things that fly in, shake around, play music, or drop in from cyberspace. Make your site easy to view and use from any device, be it desktop, laptop, notebook, or mobile phone.
- **Biographical information on your agency, the leadership, and executives** – When you're writing the copy for this, be careful. Don't spend all your time outlining the number of agencies you have and what great customer service you deliver. This is a place to show why you're credible. Put yourself in their shoes. Why should they work with you? You can highlight awards that illustrate your industry knowledge. You should talk about your years in the community and how you give back to it. You can discuss how your team's background and years of experience translates into a better experience for your clients and assures the best protection at the best possible investment.

Maybe the most important thing about web sites I can convey to you is to keep it current. I've had a web site for my consulting practice since 2005. As I write this book, I am heading into my fourth major iteration. That doesn't include minor updates about every six months. Obsolescence happens quickly in our world today and it's a cardinal sin. Dated material simply tells the reader that you aren't taking your business seriously. The comparison is like letting your agency building deteriorate by allowing weeds grow unabated, paint to fade, and ignore the broken steps leading into the front door. Your web site is now the most critical credibility statement you have. Make sure it says what you want it to!

Leveraging social media through your web site

You may have noticed that I didn't mention anything about social media and blogs on what needs to be included on your web site. That's because I've allocated a full section to it. This section is going to very specifically discuss how to leverage the social media platforms (Facebook, Twitter, LinkedIn, YouTube) through your web site and maximize its reach and message. Consider these next vignettes my ***BEST PRACTICES***...

#1 *Social media links.* Your web site should offer your reader the opportunity to link to any of your social media sites on every page. You never know when they notice it or want to learn more. It's much easier to locate on the page they are on than to be required to go back to the home page.

#2 *Have a blog*. This blog should have multiple contributors from your team – producers, customer service, claims, marketing, and leadership. Give value, don't talk about the weather. I don't have issues with occasional stories on community events and things to do in the summer. Make them the exception, not the rule. Your blog should be filled with timely topics about health care, liability risks, current events that insurance and risk management deal with, and smart ways to save premium dollars. You should be writing blogs at a minimum of two per week and aggressively promoting them on all your social media sites, your signature file on your emails, and everywhere you correspond with clients and prospects.

#3 *Social Media Coordinator.* I recommend that you as the owner find someone in your agency who is resourceful and smart in social media and delegate the *Social Media Coordinator* job to them. They will be responsible for gathering blog articles, updating daily, monitoring comments and shares, and keeping current with news. They don't need to be the author of the blogs or even the posts. They should have authority to gather all the information. By the way, a terrific way to add youth and vitality to your agency is to hire an intern (high school or college). They don't need to know the insurance business. They just need to know social media, and I promise you they will. It's a great way to introduce young, talented people to the industry. Who knows, you might hire them later full-time!

#4 *Provide your typical client results as a navigation bar*. Your clients may all differ in line of insurance, yet I bet you have typical results for all of them. These might include results like:

- Response time minimum standards
- Annual client reviews on all lines
- Monthly newsletters with cost saving and protection tips
- Web site chat with customer service

- A resource center for clients only with username and password to access important documents and information
- A free decoder ring

Well, maybe everything but the decoder ring. You get the point. Why is your client better off with you as their agent? Make sure you tell them loud and clear on your web site!

#5 *Profiles of your staff.* This should include photos, resumes, a direct link to email from their profile, access to their LinkedIn profile page and a phone number. You would do well to keep the profile brief (three paragraphs) and include personal information like family, hobbies, and pets. Why? This is a relationship business. People do business with people, not agencies. Never forget that. The more comfortable they are and the more they like who they would work with, the more likely you are to acquire them as clients. You'd be shocked (or maybe not) at the number of insurance agency web sites that seem to hide their staff not promote them – basically make them invisible. If you want to make your staff invisible, you have the wrong staff! If you think they are good, then promote your team all over your web site. Make them the reason people want to come to you.

#6 *Keep it clean.* You want your site to be attractive. Don't clutter it with unnecessary information, graphics, or Flash. Remember that people will be viewing your site on mobile devices, too. You have to make it easy and attractive to read from wherever it might be viewed.

#7 *Keep it current.* Any time you have a change, send out your own social media press release. For example, if you have a new hire, make sure their profile is quickly put on the web site and send that link out to your social media sites with an announcement. Another example might be an award your agency received. You should have a "News" navigation bar that would address this. As with the new hire, send this out to be viewed. This keeps your site fresh and informative.

Web Thought – Keep in mind that your web site is about credibility. You want people to see what they gain from being on it. Promote your web site through social media because a growing number of your prospects live on social media. Be fresh, be informative, create curiosity, and always add value to the reader. The goal is to rouse people to call you, email you, instant message you, or send a carrier pigeon to you begging for your service!

David vs. Goliath: Fighting the Internet Sales Giant

The vast majority of you reading this book are insurance agents, producers, agency principals, and insurance company executives. I'd wager that your competition at some level includes the Internet, especially if you specialize in personal lines markets, and life insurance.

> *Definition:* ***Internet Sales Giant*** – the marketing monster that feeds off television viewers, Internet surfers, radio listeners, and social media platforms. Be careful. They are often craftily disguised. They rarely use an agent; rather they are people behind a curtain who you will spin you a quote, like a spider spins a web.

> **Note**: *My definition does not include companies that offer 24/7 customer service or chat opportunities for clients. Leveraging technology to take care of your client in the manner they want to be serviced is admirable and soon to be necessary for everyone.*

You may think my definition to be cynical, and maybe you are offended. My guess is you're not a lizard or an animated character. My preference for any insurance buyer is that they deal with people they can see, feel, and barge in on when necessary. Captive carriers like Farmers, Allstate, American Family, and State Farm have fancy advertisements, yet they all highlight their agents. The *Internet Sales Giant* is the platform where consumers can "talk" with someone on the phone or via chat and quickly procure a quote and even bind coverage with little or no assistance or guidance. If you're a personal lines agent, they are your enemy.

Your challenge is that as we have described in this chapter, a preponderance of people are now so at ease with the Internet that they feel they can tackle their personal insurance there. Unfortunately, the consequences of doing that are far more worrying than booking your own travel or buying an electronic book. The thing you should most concern yourself with is not the prospect. You don't really even know who they are. You need to be concerned about your client base. They are the ones that you do know who are vulnerable to the *Giant*. In the next few pages, we will discuss what those consequences are and how you avoid letting clients be tempted.

Consequences of the ***Internet Sales Giant***: The consequences are important to you. You must be able to effectively illustrate to any of your clients who are potentially shopping the perils that they might face. How do you do this? Simple. You tell them BEFORE they start shopping. But, I digress...this is a teaser for the remainder of the chapter. First, let's look at the ***perils*** of buying personal insurance over the Internet:

1. **Limits too low**

   It's really easy to lower a rate by 35% if the liability limits is reduced. You would think this might be obvious to the insured, but I can assure you it's not. Their eyes are directly focused on the numbers that come after the dollar sign, not those on the declarations page. Don't get me wrong; I'm not implying your clients aren't smart or business savvy. What I am saying is that insurance is confusing and without a representative you can sit down and discuss this with, it's easy to lose protection.

2. **Protection lost**

   In addition to reduced limits, coverage can be lost. For example, without proper education, a coverage like Underinsured Motorist (not mandatory) can be left off in the name of saving money. The difficult part of not working with an agent is that recommendations and proactive advice can be lost. You might infer from my comments that I am denouncing the professionalism or capacity of the "agents" serving those on the other end of the phone or in chat. I'm sure these folks are trained and licensed; yet for an initial investigation into purchasing (or switching) insurance, as a sophisticated buyer you might want to know the background and expertise of these people. They are most likely on a level of commission, which does breed doing what needs to be done to close the sale. How does this differ from your "Main Street Agent?" At least if the insured is angry with the latter, she can walk in the door and demand things are dealt with. That's not likely the case with the former.

   An additional concern is the plenitude of analysis. Scheduled jewelry, personal umbrella, benefits of permanent insurance vs. term life, and other such topics of conversation might not ever occur. People may not realize they need it, but they just very well might. The only way to know is to have that discussion, and that's where you come in.

3. **Commoditization of insurance and obsolescence.**

   Personal and life insurance are unfortunately often thought of as "necessary evils" and commodities. The ability to purchase them on the Internet all by oneself adds to that mindset. The inherent vice in this thinking hurts the insured and you. The insured ends up making buying decisions with cost as the main determinant. This is dangerous on many levels. Once it is done, it's easier to forget about the insurance and allow it to become obsolete. Insurance that is out of date most often translates into insurance that does not protect. The danger to you is that you become lumped into the commodity trap and you don't want to be there. You're a well educated and licensed professional, just like any CPA, attorney, or financial professional. The image of the insurance "salesman" needs to be replaced by the trusted advisor. Trusted advisors are not related to the *Internet Sales Giant*! This is about your long-term credibility and sustainability as an agent.

How to slay the giant: As I teased you with earlier, you have control over this situation. You have the ability to influence your clientele and avoid the temptation of seeking insurance from the Giant. Here are my "Best Practices" for slaying the Giant:

1. **Don't be a stranger**

   The primary reason people leave their agents has nothing to do with price. It has to do with abandonment. When a new client buys a policy and then never hears from their agent again, that's abandonment. When the only correspondence comes annually in a letter that greets you with your formal name, rather than what you go by (e.g. Dear Daniel vs. Dear Dan), that's abandonment. When all service is doled out to the company and they have no reason to even think about you anymore, then they will abandon you.

   You don't need to be a pest or so pervasive that they can't stand you. You do need to be visible and when you are, offer them something of benefit. Here are a few ideas:

   - A short, yet interesting electronic newsletter to all clients (with their permission).
   - A personal annual review (with a phone call or visit), rather than a letter acting as a review demanding they perform the work.

- A regular mailing that has nothing to do with insurance. Maybe it's about a community service project, or upcoming local events, or maybe even the high school football scores . If you always talk about insurance, you lose a little of the relationship luster.

2. **Embrace technology**

   Make technology your partner. Be creative on your web site to allow your clients to be able to access information, get instant access, or even print out information. Technology is one of the factors appealing to people, especially your younger clientele. Use it to your advantage.

3. **Educate, educate, educate**

   You have to fight fire with fire. Keep reminding your clients of why they are better off dealing with you. Now you need to come through on your promises or else they have every reason to flee to the Giant. This education comes from your blogs, your newsletters, your conversations, and your continuous contact (spot a trend?). You can't assume they know. You must assume that they get hammered with the other message more often than you tell them. In the end, it's always about relationships. Wouldn't you rather have a date with a real, flesh and blood person, rather than a virtual online date? Give them a better time than they can get online.

Final thoughts

Technology is not something to be feared, but to be embraced. As your demographics become increasingly centered around those people that have only known technology in their lives, that communicate almost solely through technology, and who have no idea what yellow pages are, then you have to adapt or die. Look at the newspaper industry as an example. If you commit to providing your clients with unparalleled value, then you will end up with a retention rate that is the envy of your competitors. Make sure you're using the high touch aspects of hi tech to achieve it.

Chapter 5

Stop Cold Calling

Seven more effective and efficient ways to market insurance

Why interruption marketing is bad for them and you

Nobody likes to be bothered at the dinner table with an unsolicited phone call or knock on the door. When I was young, being interrupted at night by a solicitor was about the worst thing you could do to my father. He literally just hung up the phone and walked away muttering angrily. There was never a chance of acquiring business or influencing him in any way using this method.

Today in our personal and business lives, we are inundated with SPAM in our emails, we are pitched to purchase "can't miss stock plays" on the telephone, and now are getting SPAM on our text messaging. There must be some people buying products this way because the interruption marketers keep doing it. What I can tell you with absolute certainty is this – the clients you want to acquire and retain in your book of business do not like it. This is true for commercial, personal, and life/health/disability lines prospects.

When I first started in the agency business in 1989, my boss sent me over to Safeco Insurance for a three-day, intensive producer training. Along with several other "newbies," we memorized scripts to cold call personal lines prospects at night. We rehearsed how to overcome objections, how to engage in conversations, and how to influence them to take a quote. In the evening session, we would literally sit with a phone book and dial for dollars. We had no idea whom we were calling, if they were a good prospect, or what we were interrupting them from. It was a detestable experience and I hated every minute of it. It was part of the brainwashing that the law of large numbers applied to cold calling as well as actuarial analysis.

The biggest thing I learned in the experience is that the people who actually took a few minutes to talk with me and wanted a quote were never a good prospect. They had other insurance issues that made them interested in what you were pitching.

They had non-renewals, cancellations, poor driving records, and dilapidated homes. They shopped on price only and generally ended up wasting everyone's time, which is an irony in itself. The people you did want to insure never talked to you. They had mediocre to solid relationships with agents that didn't take them away from dinner or valuable time with their family. In the end, it was clear that cold calling was the right term for what we were doing. The majority of our experience was frigid, and the results were poor. Overall, it was a terrible waste of time and money. In the end, dialing for dollars equated to adverse selection!

Commercial lines cold calling is no different. In nearly 17 years as an agent, I walked in "cold" to a lot of businesses, trying to meet the owner or decision maker. To say I didn't have some modicum of success would not be true, because I did. But the reality is that from an efficiency standpoint, it was a poor way of doing things. If I were an agent today, I would definitely do things differently. As I will outline in this chapter, building relationships and developing the trust it takes to write insurance for people and businesses usually result from better ways.

Your goals in marketing should be two-fold. First, you want a meeting with the decision maker. Second, you want to maximize the time you spend marketing. You want the highest return for your time investment. Cold calling is a bad method to accomplish both of these goals, especially the latter.

Definition – "Cold calling" in my book is truly icy and dicey. You are calling on (either on the phone or in person) someone whom you have no reason to contact other than the fact they have warm blood surging through their veins. When I used to call on potential new clients that I had never met, I tried to add some "warmth" to the equation. These folks were either members of an association that I had the recommendation from, they were part of a buying group where I had testimonials from peers, or they were referred to me. By having some reason to call on them that allows for association, you are warming up your call and have more credibility than if you just walk in off the street.

Where do you get your business?

There are really only four ways that insurance agents find new clients. There may be a few stragglers, but these four ways make up at least 95% of your new business opportunities.

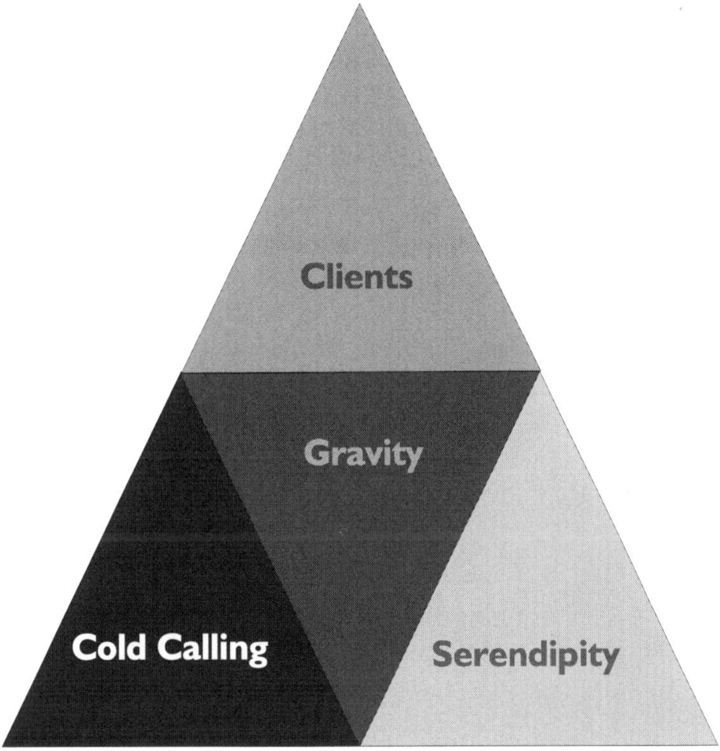

Cold calling is by far the *worst* method of gaining new clients yet it's where most agents spend an inordinate amount of their time. It's the least efficient, most intrusive, and leads to more rejection than anything else. I put this in the lower left quadrant as the technique you should do the least. I know this is a huge paradigm shift for many of you. So like a 3-pack a day smoker trying to quit, you don't have to go cold turkey. Just start cutting back and being more intentional on the cold calling you do.

Cold calling should be left to very targeted markets. If you have a specialty like long-term care, technology-driven companies, or amusement park business, then target those businesses and give yourself a fighting chance. As you will see later on in this chapter, I believe it makes sense to find referrals into these cold calls to heat them up. If you must cold call, then be smart and thoughtful about it. Don't just start throwing darts and seeing what sticks.

Serendipity is great, but you just can't count on it. Sometimes business will literally just fall into your lap. Serendipity is being in the right place at the right time; simply just luck. We often make our own luck.

When I was still an agent, I had been working on insuring a nice funeral home operation. This was a family-owned business and I had gone to college with one of the sons who was eventually going to be taking over the business from his father. I wasn't sure that he was the decision-maker, but I knew he had influence. I made my best play, but came up short. I was pretty sure that David wanted to go with me, but I had not yet earned the trust of his brother and co-partner. David's parting words were, "Don't give up on us. We will eventually be working together."

I was disappointed, yet not dissuaded. I sent him a nice thank-you card for his time and went about setting up a follow-up for the next year. A week later, David called (a day before it renewed) and said, "We've changed our mind. We want to move our business to you!" Turns out the thank-you card had a bigger effect than I had imagined. They were so taken (including his brother, Mark), with me sending the card that they decided I offered a better relationship than the one they had. I kept them as a client until I left to start my consulting practice, and then kept them as a client after that. I still work with them today.

You might argue that this wasn't serendipity. That the work I put in on the account paved the way. While this may be partly true, I never expected a thank-you card to have that impact, and I've never had another situation where it immediately paid dividends like this. I was a bit lucky.

You can't count on thank-you cards and blind referrals being part of your long-term sustainability. They will always play a small part, and should be considered. But you can't really impact them outside of being active in the next two categories.

Gravity is marketing gravity. By dint of your activity in shamelessly promoting and branding yourself and your company, opportunities will fall down to the earth like Isaac Newton's apple. Here is a list of marketing gravity activities that will reap rewards for you…

- Press releases about your awards, achievements, and activities
- Social media activity
- Pro Bono work
- Publishing – articles, blogs, executive briefs
- Video clips used on your web site
- Testimonials
- Public speaking
- Webinars, podcasts, and teleconferences
- Web sites

Gravity is about making you the first to come to mind in your industry. If you're the locally recognized thought leader on insurance, then people will naturally gravitate to you. In my experience, agents have been poor at doing this type of work. I will admit I have seen some improvement, but it is slow in coming. Agents and brokers will do well to slide a chunk of their cold calling time over to this area. It will reap bigger, quicker, and more consistent rewards.

Clients are the pinnacles of where you get new business. Referrals are the lifeblood of any business, and you as an agent are your own business entity, whether you own your agency, are a producer for a company or agency, or if you work as a company executive or representative. The next chapter will be dedicated to maximizing this most important method of new business acquisition. For now, let's look at my 7-Step program for achieving marketing success.

The 7 Steps

If I were still an agent today, I would go about marketing to acquire clients in a wholly different way. I've learned a great deal on professional services marketing from my years as a consultant. For me, this was a huge culture shift because much of it bucked the conventional wisdom that I was trained and educated (brainwashed) in. I would focus on the ***7 Steps*** to better marketing that maximize your time and gain you better access to meet and influence decision makers.

Step #1 – Publishing

This book you're reading is an example of how publishing leads to opportunity. You've either been given or purchased this book. Since this is Chapter 5, you've been influenced enough and gained enough value to keep reading to this point.

Publishing can, but doesn't exclusively mean, a book. Both commercially published and self-published books have value. That being said, insurance and risk management aren't always the sexiest topics for your clients, so a book might not make sense. What might make sense, however, is the plethora of ways you can get your value out to prospects in more bite-sized chunks that they are more willing to digest.

Executive briefs are short (hence the name) articles of generally 4-5 pages that focus on a specific topic. They can be read in less than 10 minutes yet can pack a powerful punch for your client. They should raise an issue of a critical nature, discuss the peril to the prospect, and then offer a solution.

Example: You could write an executive brief on the peril of cyber crime in today's volatile world of business technology. Cyber crime has the potential to ruin your client's reputation, cost them a ton of money, and suspend their operations. This is a fairly new risk to business owners and their level of sophistication is not too great at this point. You would be posing a new idea to them. In your executive brief, you can lay out the dangers and loss of opportunity that a business owner faces due to this peril. You can provide case studies and industry statistics to back up your point. And, you can bring the danger to life by highlighting the consequences in their own world. Then, you can provide the good news. You can illustrate how to solve this issue through strong risk management practices. You can discuss strategy and techniques, risk transfer methods, and help them understand education and training for employees. This is not a pitch for you. Rather, it's an example of the value you bring your clients. If you send out one of these every quarter to your prospect base, I guarantee you will be providing more consistent value to them than their own agents are.

Blogs are an easy and effective way to offer pithy, yet substantive value to your prospects and clients. Blogs are meant to be short – one to three paragraphs. You can discuss and wax poetic on timely topics and issues, offer your sage advice, and/or simply give your opinion on something unrelated to the news or risk management in general. I've seen some agencies that are doing a terrific job of getting into the fray. They've attached a blog to their web site and ask the agents to contribute regularly. Now, the web site has added value that can remain timely and laden with value for the visitor. It also is a good way to invite people to visit your web site when you're at marketing and networking events.

Example: EHL Insurance (a subsidiary of Brown & Brown Insurance) is an agency just outside of Seattle, Washington. They have assembled a team of bloggers in their agency. Each team member has a specific area of expertise, such as employee benefits, risk management, and business development. They take turns contributing stories for the blog, making sure there is consistency in posts. In addition, they've made it possible for readers to share the blog through social media channels. This is free for them to produce, costs really nothing more than a little time and creativity, and adds tremendous value to those who read it. Even more importantly, it's another reason to have a conversation with a new prospect.

I interviewed Jason Mayer from EHL Insurance. Jason is a producer, risk manager, principal, and a contributing blogger for the agency. I asked him about the genesis of EHL's blog.

"It came out of the desire to become better known to our clients and prospects as an expert in their core area of focus, which is risk management and insurance," said Mr. Mayer. "I want them to read my blog and say, '*Hey, I need to talk to Jason!*'"

Mr. Mayer says that Search Engine Optimization (SEO) was also a factor is starting the blog. The hope is that when prospects are doing research on them as a company and use any search engine, their name and blog will appear.

EHL uses a team of contributing bloggers to keep the pipeline moving. They have a marketing coordinator within the agency to make sure people are contributing and that all focus areas are being addressed. The blogging is fairly new and results are still unclear. However, EHL is committed to keeping up their part of the bargain by putting out important insurance and risk management information to their clients and prospects. They have also made it a valuable tool within their web site.

Newsletters are a great way to keep up a presence with your clients. I encourage electronic emails, rather than hard copy, because it is much less expensive. Newsletters have traditionally been used as a way to stay in contact with your clients and help with retention. That is still the case. However, there are ways you can maximize your newsletter as an outreach to prospects.

Example: Ask prospects if they'd like to receive your newsletter to learn more about ways they can save money on their insurance. Carry around a few hard copies of newsletter (and blog) articles that you can give them during networking opportunities. Ask them if they would mind being interviewed for your newsletter, and then sign them up. Newsletters may not appear to lead directly to new business but what they do is build your credibility, enhance your brand, and help put you in a "top of mind" category when someone starts thinking about their insurance. And that is exactly where you want to be!

Step #2 - Public Speaking

There is an old Jerry Seinfeld comedy routine where he quips that the #1 fear of people is public speaking and death is ranked as #2. He postulates that at a funeral, most people would choose to be in the casket, rather than giving the eulogy!

Outside of referrals, I get the majority of my business from speaking. I work hard to find opportunities to speak at events and conferences where decision makers will be attending. My goal is to always have at least two people come up to me after and say, "Dan, we need to talk!" Insurance agents are missing the boat on speaking. My perception is that they:

1. lack the confidence to speak well in public
2. don't know what to talk about
3. think they will be viewed as "pitching"
4. have no idea where to speak
5. don't understand how it can make them money

Lack of confidence

Lack of confidence is the #1 reason people don't want to speak in public for any reason. They fear the eyes upon them and there is a fear that they might be "found out," or look goofy, or be laughed at. Fear is something an insurance agent better overcome in any aspect of the job, or it will be a short-lived career.

The best way to boost your confidence is through practice. Fortunately, there are many ways to practice!

When I first started my consulting practice, I knew that speaking was going to be an important part of building my credibility and brand. Speaking had never been an issue for me. I was comfortable speaking in front of groups, and had been at one time early in my career a member of Toastmasters. I prided myself on speaking well extemporaneously, on telling good stories, and in uncovering humor to help people laugh while they were learning.

As I began finding speaking opportunities, I also began to realize I was not as good as I thought. You see, confidence does not always equate to competence. And when you realize that competence isn't what you thought it was, confidence goes out the window quickly! I remember speaking once to Chamber of Commerce crowd. I found myself feeling unprepared, using notes, and quite frankly being downright boring. This was a truly humbling experience. I decided to get back into Toastmasters.

> Toastmasters International is in my estimation, the most inexpensive and powerful organization you can belong to in order to bolster the most important business skill you need to have – speaking. It provides you with a safe environment to

fail; excellent feedback and suggestions for improvement, and above all, Stage Time. One of my speaking mentors is Darren LaCroix (2001 World Champion of Public Speaking), and "Stage Time" is his mantra. The more opportunities you get to speak in public, the better you will get regardless of how it turned out. Toastmasters is an easy, simple, and powerful way for anyone to become a better speaker and enhance their career.

Long story short – my speaking improved dramatically. It was like jumping back on a bicycle after having not ridden in 20 years. I ended up seeking out even more sophisticated coaching though the likes of Darren LaCroix and other top speaking coaches. You don't need to do that. You just need to be confident, polished, and prepared. You need the tools to bring in humor, personal stories, and metaphor. You can do all of that through an organization like Toastmasters and put yourself in a position above where the vast majority of your competitors are, and that is nowhere. Note however that if you want to rise above the crowd and be truly influential, hiring a coach to help you makes sense and will return your investment many times over.

Speaking to buying groups, associations, civic groups, and other potential clients will put you in a much better stead that talking into their office or calling them uninvited. You've gone from frigid to warm without even trying!

Step #3 – Press releases

This seems like a simple thing, but in all honesty, individual agents rarely do it. Agency owners might have a "marketing department" somewhere in the office that occasionally sends these notices out, but they are rarely doing it consistently. Press releases are simple (build a template), inexpensive (free), and get you great exposure (people read them). Here's an easy to implement system for agency owners of any size to immediately use.

1. **Create a template.** Once you have a template in place, you literally just plug and play with future releases. The key components of a good press release are as follows:
    - Eye catching headline
    - Date and location of release
    - Right-to-the-point opening paragraph
    - Informative, well-written paragraph
    - Testimonial (if suitable)

- Contact information including phone number, email, and web site.
- Three hash tags – ### – to indicate to the editor that the press release is done

Here is a sample press release for your review…

Dan Weedin Inducted into Million Dollar Consultant™ Hall of Fame

Poulsbo, WA (November 15, 2012) – Dan Weedin, a Seattle-area based insurance consultant, executive coach, and speaker, was formally inducted into the Million Dollar Consultant™ Hall of Fame on November 13th. He was one of five consultants of diverse disciplines to be awarded this honor.

Alan Weiss, Ph.D. announced the honors during his annual Mentor Summit held at the Mandarin Oriental Hotel in San Francisco, CA. Dr. Weiss is the author of Million Dollar Consulting and over 40 other books in the field of consulting, coaching, and speaking. He conducts a global mentoring program for consultants and holds multiple awards in the consulting and speaking professions.

Criteria for being inducted in this elite group include:

- Serving as an exemplar to others in the profession.
- Manifesting the highest levels of integrity, ethics, and accountability.
- Achieving significant annual revenue and profit improvement.
- Contributing intellectual capital to the consulting profession.
- Engaging in continuing, challenging, personal and professional development.
- Taking prudent risk and demonstrating resilience.

Alan Weiss says, "Dan Weedin exemplifies our Hall of Fame through his generous sharing, community support, business growth, and high integrity. He is constantly asking, 'How can I help my clients improve?' trusting that they will always provide positive rewards for him, as well."

Also inducted in this class were Scott Wintrip (St. Petersburg, FL), Steven Bleistein (Tokyo), Bart Sayle (United Kingdom), and Judy Chan (San Francisco). Honorees are chosen from the global participants in the Private Roster Mentor Program, who number well over 1,000.

Weedin is an expert in crisis leadership and insurance, and helps his clients to maximize their ability to respond and thrive out of crisis. He also coaches and mentors individual consultants and insurance professionals to help them achieve greater success in their careers.

For more information, contact Dan Weedin at (360) 271-1592; (360) 824-8100 (fax); or dan@weedin.com. Please also visit our website at www.DanWeedin.com.

###

2. **Create a position**. In an agency, I recommend you find one central person to handle the duties of sending out press releases. Once this person has the process down, she can be in charge of consistently asking for news and information from everyone in the agency. She can be the main contact person for the media, become the resident expert, and create a consistency that is needed to leverage the power of this free marketing practice.
3. **Educate your team on what is press release worthy.** There is actually a lot that happens in your agency that is press release "worthy." You just haven't thought about it in these terms. Editors eschew anything that is overtly promotional or viewed as "pitching" your business. They want items that are informative, educational, and promotional in a sense of achievement. Check out Visual 6.1 to see a list of ideas that your press release guru can utilize and twist arms for…

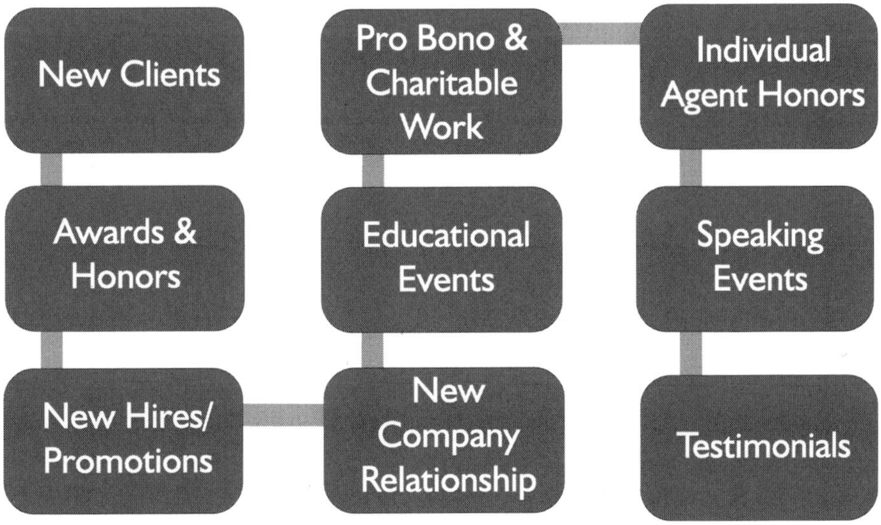

As you can see, there is plenty to keep your guru busy! Press releases are especially effective in local communities. If you're a small agency (under 15 employees) in a community, your constituency will read the local papers, follow on the Internet, and keep up with the local news. Being ubiquitous is good for your brand, good for your repute, and good for your business!

Step # 4 – Intentional networking

You might be wondering why I would use the term "intentional" when defining this style of marketing. Isn't all networking intentional? Not really. Cold calling, albeit intentional on your part, is just a shotgun approach to marketing. You fire off as many rounds as possible and see what falls out of the sky. My definition of intentional marketing is much different.

Being intentional in your marketing is NOT:

- handing out an unlimited number of business cards to people who will soon dump them in the trash.
- attending events that don't include your target audience (e.g. economic buyers).
- walking into rooms and not having a strategy or minimum expectations.
- being unprepared to offer your value to others rather than just your job title.

Here is a game plan you should use for developing a networking plan. It's easy to accomplish, yet it does require that you spend time planning and strategizing. Too many insurance agents go bounding off like dogs after the hunt without the least understanding of what their goals are or how they measure them.

Step 1: Know your value proposition. When someone asks you what you do, your standard answer probably is, "I'm an insurance agent." That rarely leads to an inspired conversation on the value of life insurance, auto insurance, or the quality of the food on your plate. Being an insurance agent is a methodology, not a value. People want to know what's in it for them. Your value proposition should sound more like, "I protect my client's lifestyle for the rest of their life." This is a real value. Let's conjecture on how an ideal conversation might sound like:

Prospect: So, what do you do?
You: I protect my client's lifestyle for the rest of their life.
Prospect: Wow. That's an interesting statement. What does that mean?

> *You*: That is pretty ambiguous, isn't it? How about this? Instead of being theoretical, tell me a little bit about your business/family/life (pick one) and then I might be better able to discuss how we could work together.

The goal is to get the prospect talking, not you! Insurance agents have the reputation for doing a lot of talking about what they do and how they do it. The emphasis should actually be on why the prospect needs you and how you show them your value to improve their condition.

Your goal should be to create a compelling value proposition that highlights results for your client, not your job title. Then ask provocative questions and allow them to talk, not you!

Step 2: Determine your min/max. This is a concept I learned from my professional mentor, Alan Weiss. Alan taught me that going into any situation – meeting, networking event, speech, etc. – you need to know in advance what your minimum objective is, and what your maximum expectation is. Here's an example…

I have a meeting with the owner of a 140-person business and an insurance agent whom I collaborate with has referred me to him. The meeting is set up as a lunch with the economic buyer and two subordinates, along with my endorser (always the best referral). My minimum expectation out of this lunch meeting is a second meeting. I know that lunches aren't usually ideal to get the information I need for a proposal, so I want to create enough interest to meet again. My maximum expectation is that he hires me on the spot. This is unlikely, but if it happens then my maximum goal is attained. In this example, we had a terrific meeting, Steve (the buyer) got to know me, and we decided that we were going to work together at some capacity, and scheduled the next meeting right then and there. My minimum was met, and actually expanded as the decision to work with me moved from "if" to "how."

This is how it should work with you. Every engagement in intentional marketing needs to have some metric of success at a minimum and maximum level. Consider you're at a networking event for a Chamber of Commerce. These situations are laden with business card hucksters, as if the person who doles out the most cards wins. You should plan on being more strategic. Perhaps at a minimum, you want to gain one new appointment with a prospective buyer. At a maximum, you want three contacts that will immediately lead to appointments. Once you hit your minimum, the rest is gravy. Once you hit your maximum, stuff another crab puff in your mouth and head home! You've met your goal, so there is no reason to stick around and waste time. Be intentional and honest with your objectives.

Step #5 – Non-profit community work

Your work in non-profit and charitable arenas should be genuine. Don't ever blur the lines of true philanthropy and marketing. Find a cause that means something to you and that you truly believe in. Then find a way to become active in it, especially on a board level. While you are helping advance the cause of your charity, you are creating relationships and meeting other philanthropic people who would benefit from working with you.

You must be smart in these situations. Just in off-hand conversations, you will be asked about your business. You will undoubtedly ask others about theirs. Be attentive, be interested, and ask questions. At an appropriate moment, especially away from the work of the charity, find a time to inquire about a meeting to see if there is any synergy. There is nothing wrong with offering expertise to those you know.

I've been in Rotary now for 20 years with two fantastic clubs. That involvement has spanned two distinct careers as both an insurance agent and a consultant. I've never actually kept track, but my best guess is that over those 20 years, a good 70% of my business came as a result, in some way, of being part of Rotary. That includes directly working with my fellow Rotarians as my clients, being referred by a Rotarian to someone else, and meeting someone in a different city who was a Rotarian and recognized the pin I wear on my suit coats and sports jackets. This business has been a by-product of work in Rotary. I believe in the service club's mission and values and I have been active in leadership roles, the youth exchange program, and many a work party where you roll up your sleeves and work side by side on a project. Most Rotarians I know do business together. It comes from sitting with each other weekly to break bread and become trusted friends and partners.

Find one cause to promote and advance. Care about it for personal reasons. Volunteer your time and donate your money. And meet people along the way who would make good clients and talk to them about their situations.

Step#6 – Webinars and teleconferences

This tactic has become a staple of mine in my consulting practice. In fact, as I write this chapter, just yesterday I hosted a webinar for over 40 insurance professionals in the Western United States on the topic of referrals (next chapter). Webinars and teleconferences are almost free to create, run, record, and distribute. Here's what the process looks like:

Pick a topic

You have a ton to pick from including cyber liability, employment practices liability, health care reform, long-term care, social media and insurance, or how to save money on your personal insurance.

Find a platform

This means choose among one of the following – webinar, teleconference, podcast, or even streaming video. These are all either free or virtually free to use. If you're even just slightly technically inclined (you know, you can send a text message), then you should be able to figure these out. If not, find the nearest teenager and pay them to teach you. It's worth the investment.

Shamelessly promote

Tell everyone. Send out press releases, promote on social media, send emails to your mailing list, and hire your local Pony Express rider to spread the word. There are way too many easy ways to toot your horn. Make sure that you're tooting it on behalf of the message and not you. The promotion should be clearly about how the audience you want to attract will receive value. Make it about them and they are more likely to come.

Event

Hold the event. Make it free, or almost free. You will attract more people that way. Record it if you can to include on your web site later. Be good. That means you need to practice public speaking skills. Just because you're like the mighty Oz behind the curtain, doesn't mean you can get away with being boring.

Follow up

Make sure you gather names and email addresses for your attendees. Send them something free after the event. It might be slides that you used, visuals, surveys, articles, or decoder rings. Whatever it is, make sure they get something in addition as a sign of gratitude. If I were you, I would offer a free 15-minute consultation. Find some way to begin to create a relationship and a buzz.

Step #7 – Alliances

I have a good friend and colleague named Libby Wagner. Libby and I first met at a National Speakers Association event where we went to watch internationally renowned speaker coach, Patricia Fripp present at the Starbucks Corporate offices. From that meeting, our paths continued to cross as we found ourselves as part of the same global community. As we didn't have competing practices, we respected each other's work, and we wanted to help each other out, a close friendship emerged and we kept in constant contact.

In 2010, Alan Weiss started what he called his Master Mentor program. It was a program where he would train consultants and coaches to excel in mentoring other consultants. Both Libby and I applied, were accepted, and were trained by Alan. At the time, we were the only Master Mentors in the Northwest.

About a year later, Libby and I got together over lunch and had a brainstorm. What if we pooled our resources, efforts, and community to host an event where we could help consultants and at the same time, look to acquire new clients? We had been going it alone in the marketing process, and although successful, wanted to continue to grow. The idea was that if we offered an event with outstanding value to a larger group, we could expand our brands and visibility. Thus was born Libby & Dan.

As I write this book, we have held two events. We each have added numerous new clients from those two events. In addition, we have been able to strengthen existing relationships and increase our brand by adding each other's community to ours. This alliance has been beneficial for both if us. We each gained new clients. We each enhanced our brand and expanded our visibility. And we each improved our own skills and ability to hold excellent events. Our new clients and attendees benefited from their participation through new skills and enhanced networking opportunities. I guess this is what you would call a win-win-win.

Alliances come in many forms. In my situation with Libby, we created an event, planned out a marketing strategy, took a risk, and delivered. The results are listed above. How can you as an insurance agency use the power of alliances to acquire new business? Easy Find partners who are non-competing where together, you can be mutually beneficial to each other and to your clients. Here are a few examples…

Real Estate Agents: If you're a personal lines agent, form an alliance with the best real estate agent in your market. Provide them with resources to help their clientele. This might include:

- Short articles on how to purchase insurance for your new home

- Dangers and traps to beware of for both property and liability claims
- How to save money on homeowners insurance

Ask your alliance partner to hand these out to all of their clients, not in an effort to pitch you, but to offer them value. What's in it for them, you may ask? If the information is good and their clients receive value and like them, they are viewed as the nexus of information.

CPAs: These are highly important people to business owners. They often have in-depth discussions about risk and protecting their investments. As with the example above, create resources for these CPAs to give to their clients. Make the CPA a hero and help their clients, and you will get opportunities.

- Others:
- Bankers
- Wealth managers
- Consultants
- Attorneys
- Other agents whose specialties are different than yours
- Association executives

Bottom line: Cold-calling stinks on all accounts for you. Your batting average will drop way below the Mendoza Line*, you are likely to annoy your best prospects and be like a magnet to those you don't want on your books, and you will have wasted valuable time that could have been spent on any of the seven techniques I listed above. I tend to be an "old school" kind of guy, but in the case of cold calling, class is dismissed!

Mendoza Line – Former Seattle Mariners baseball player Mario Mendoza has the dubious distinction of being a poor hitter. His batting average dipped well below the .200 mark and set an ignominious metric for futility. As a lifelong, suffering fan of the Mariners, I had to include Mr. Mendoza's woeful statistic along with the equally woeful practice of cold calling!

Chapter 6

The Rare Art of the Referral

Why you're losing it and why you need to get it back

Everyone agrees that referrals are the platinum standard for gaining new clients. It doesn't matter if you're selling insurance, real estate, or dynamite sticks. Getting a warm and friendly introduction from a trusted colleague gives you a greater chance for a meeting, an increased likelihood of giving a quote or being part of a Request for Proposal (RFP), and, ultimately, a greater chance of closing the deal. All this without the laborious chore of cold calling, begging, pleading, and/or groveling.

Acquiring new clients and customers is the hardest part of this business. It's why young agents fail and old agents retire early. It takes perseverance, a thick skin, and a little luck. The sad part is that the quickest way to success in building your business and sales pipeline is the one that gets abandoned by many. It's the simple act of asking for referrals.

Why are you losing it?

I believe there are just a few reasons why insurance agents resist asking for referrals. The common denominator revolves around lack of confidence. You might be asking, "Lack of confidence?? Hey, I have to have confidence just to get the account. Why would I lack confidence in asking for referrals?" It's a good question. Here are your answers:

1. **You fear rejection.** It's one thing to get rejected by someone you don't know, it's quite another to get rejected by a client, colleague, or friend. The fear that their response to you will come up empty and leave you walking away with your tail between your legs has many agents scared to ask.

2. **You doubt the strength of your relationship.** You are concerned that you don't know them well enough, or that they don't have enough

experience with you as their agent, to ask for a referral. In other words, you haven't fully gained their trust even though you've gained their check.

3. **You don't want to burden them.** If you really feel like a peer and trusted advisor, this isn't an issue. If you feel this way, you've put yourself into a subordinate role and this is never good for long-term client retention. This is your problem, not theirs.
4. **You don't know how to ask.** Perhaps you've never been trained properly. You have no mentor, coach, or confidante. This is just laziness and lack of desire. There are hundreds of books floating around the Internet that can teach you something about referral asking. Some of them might even be good! There are many marketing experts and coaches that can also help you (beware that you know how to hire a coach or mentor – more on that later). But there is no reason you can't learn for yourself. In the end, it's like the groundhog afraid to see it's own shadow. You don't want to learn because you will then be forced to use it and face...possible rejection. It's a vicious circle!

You lose it if you're never properly trained, if you don't practice and learn, and if you are afraid of rejection. Once you get out of the habit of asking for referrals, it's hard to jump back on. The crazy thing is you end up going back to knocking on doors and making phone calls, all of which result in more rejection and more wasted time.

Whom do you ask?

The better a referral source knows the person they are referring, the better it is for you to have a successful outcome.

The three best sources in ascending order are:

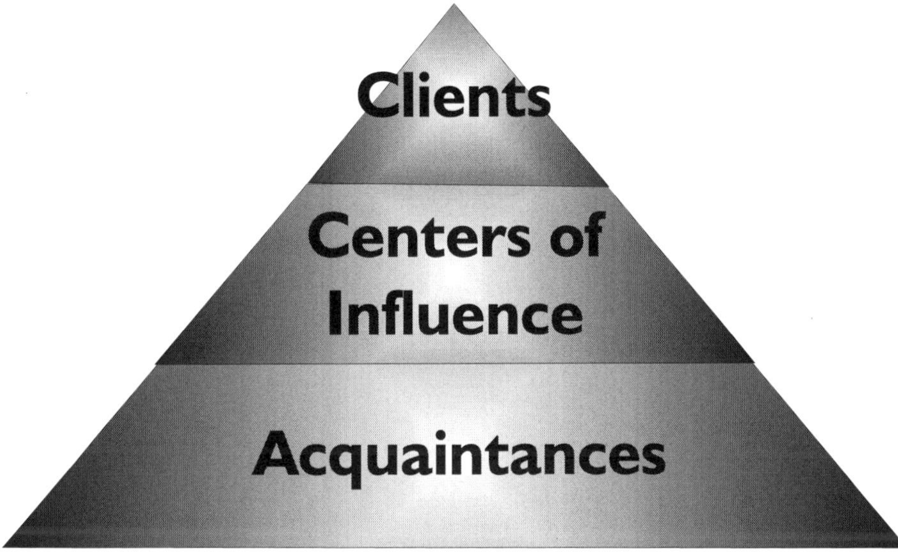

Acquaintances: These are people who are not clients, but may be a good source of referrals. This list includes family, friends, neighbors, social members, and people you do business with on a regular basis (doctor, dentist, stock broker, car repair, etc.). These people should all be aware of what you do and how you help improve the lives and conditions of others.

I can hear you as I write this - "I don't want to ask people who are in this category. They are going to think I'm just a slimy sales person. They know what I do and if they ever want to refer, that's fine." Welcome back to low self-confidence.

The only way they will think of you as a "slimy sales person" is if you act like one. If you truly believe you can help people or businesses improve their financial outlook, protect their family and business, be a trusted strategist, and help them keep costs down, then you will display this belief with your words and body language. ***The first sale is to yourself.*** If you are nervous, anxious or, even worse, embarrassed, then you will not be asking with the level of confidence needed to successfully get referrals. But if you have that strong sense of belief that you are the best thing that your friend's referral can use to help them protect their most valuable assets, then you will be successful in getting strong referrals.

Centers of influence are those people who can refer you to your target market with skill and persuasion because they are a nexus for introductions. Centers of influence tend to be other professionals who work with your target market and will have strength behind their name. Here is a short list of possible centers of influence...

- CPAs

- Attorneys
- Bankers
- Real estate agents
- Trade association executive directors
- Consultants
- Other insurance agents (who may specialize in one area and not yours. For example your center of influence only sells life insurance and you're a property and casualty agent).

Centers of influence tend to be active in giving and desiring referral business. This most definitely should be a two-way street. These folks tend to know everyone and if you do an excellent job of describing your market, they will give you names. Be aware that you need to "give to get." Be aware of what they do and how they might solve challenges for your clients and be quick to refer them.

> I recently met with a coaching client who needed help with human resources. He has about 20 employees, but no dedicated HR staff. He was ending up doing most of the HR work and this stole his time as President of his business, which is a commercial general contractor. At our regular meetings, he shared with me his frustration. Fortunately, I have a colleague who is an expert in human resources and works with small businesses. I immediately sent out an email introduction over LinkedIn as we sat there. My generosity in giving will most assuredly be reciprocated at some time in the future.

Clients are the highest peak of the referral mountain. They've personally worked with you, have seen the benefit of your services, and have by far the most credibility with others because of that work. The fact that so few agents ask for referrals of their clients is staggering to me.

How do I know they don't? Two ways – first, they tell me. My clients that I coach and mentor freely confess that they seldom to never ask for referrals. They like getting them, know they should make it a habit, yet don't do it. We generally find that the culprit is one of the reasons I detailed above. Second – in the 8 years (at the time if this writing in 2013) that I have worked closely with insurance buyers, I can count on one hand the number of times an agent asked me for a referral. I've worked in unison with agents, hired them for clients, and even given many of them praise for their work! This should be a conversation starter! Unfortunately, either through lack of preparation, not being in the moment, or plain old fear, I see agents continually walking away from potential business because they didn't ask.

The HOW

In this section, I want you to walk away from this chapter with language that you can effectively use to garner referrals, and a few best practices to keep in mind.

Here are a few of my favorite ways to ask. You need to find your comfort zone. We all have different personalities, and some methods are more comfortable than others. That being said, you should have three regular "scripts" that you use to influence a referral from either a client, center of influence, or acquaintance.

Blind ask

"Referrals are the coinage of my realm. Whom do you know that would benefit from speaking with me?"

"I build my business one great client at a time…just like with you. Who do you know that would gain benefit from talking with me?"

"I have room in my current book of business to add new clients. My best opportunities come from referrals from my best clients. Is there someone in your world that would benefit from meeting me?"

"I'm so glad you've had a great experience with our agency. Who do you know in your industry that would benefit from working with us as you've done?"

Research-based

"I understand you're a colleague of John Smith. His business is ideal for the type of work I do. Would you be willing to introduce us?"

"Thank you for entrusting your life insurance with me. You come from a large family. Would you be willing to introduce me to your siblings so they can benefit as you are?"

"I understand you and Jane Gordon serve together on the Rotary board of directors. I've been trying to meet her. Would you be willing to introduce us?"

"I saw that Bill Sherman gave you a nice recommendation on LinkedIn. Bill has a business that I'm well suited to help. Would you be willing to introduce us?

These two segments will make up the majority of your referral asking. You're either going to ask an open-ended referral (Blind Ask), or you will be very specific (Research-Based). As you can tell, the language is similar, the concept three-fold...

1. You want referrals. This starts or continues the education process for your referral network.

2. You give them guidance as to whom they want to meet.

3. You ask for the introduction.

Along the way, you've also confirmed their delight with you. Why wouldn't they endorse you?

You are only going to receive so many answers to your request. You should be prepared for all of them. The key issue here is that you are not (repeat NOT) asking them to market you. You want to be the one to do that. You simply want permission to use their name! Here are the "objections" you will hear:

Them: "Hmm. Great question. Let me think about it."

You: "That's fine, Jim. I know I may have caught you unaware. I will call you back next Monday at 9:30. Will that give you enough time to think about someone?"

Them: "I can't think of anyone right now, but if I do, I will let you know."

You: "Thanks, that's very kind. I bet there is someone you work with that you might not be thinking about as needing my help? Would it be okay if I gave you what an ideal client might look like and then get back to you next week?"

Them: "I will call Jane and see if she is interested. If she is, I will have her call you."

You: "That's very nice, but it would be unfair to have you put in the position of marketing me. It would be better for me to contact her directly and use the strength of your name."

Them: "I'd be nervous to do that since they might already have a good relationship with their agent. Why don't I ask them first and let you know?"

You: "That certainly is a good possibility and that is fine. It never hurts to chat. I promise I won't try to pitch or sell your friend. I only want to meet new and interesting people."

Don't allow your potential referrers to draw conclusions or make assumptions about your intent or what their friend/colleague is thinking. You want to be the one making the introductory call, not the prospect. You want to be the one to market yourself because there is no one better to do that. Your primary goal is to get a name, contact information, and permission to use a name. If your referrer is more assertive and introduces you personally, all the better. Just always be prepared for "objections" and have language ready to counter it.

How to effectively follow up

So, you've got the referral and you've reached out to the prospect. You've either left a voice mail, a message with a gatekeeper (and they are always in your court), or you've sent an email. Now, all you have to do is sit back and wait for the flood of people busting down your door, right?

If your experience is like mine, that's not the case. You'd like to think that by the strength of the name you dropped, that callbacks and email replies are the norm. They are not. These prospects have an idea of why you called. You can never be fully sure of the strength of the name of the person who referred you, so that is not a given. And in most cases, my guess is that people get pretty busy and even if the relationship with the referrer is rock solid, you didn't make it to the top of the priority list. And then some people simply are just rude.

You need to always remember that you are in charge of driving the referral bus. Many agents are pretty good at asking for referrals and then even making that first salvo. Much too often however, they back off after no initial response and then become either very tentative, or are scared off. This is where you need that strong self-confidence.

This part of the referral process is about "science." Let's take a look at the process of strong and confident follow up.

Voice Mail: You left a voice mail directly with the prospect. It should have sounded something like this, *"Ms. Jones, my name is Dan Weedin from Toro Insurance. Jim Smith gave me your name to contact. Jim and I have worked closely on dramatically improving his ability to continue business in the face of any crisis. He thought it would benefit both of us to meet. Please call me at 360-697-1058 (repeat), so we can find a time on our schedules. I look forward to meeting you."*

Your whole goal in this call (which you should have scripted out in front of you and have practiced) is threefold:

1. Introduce yourself and name your referrer
2. Briefly explain why you were referred. This should be a value proposition or value received by your referrer.
3. Suggest that you meet

Basically, it's a who/why/when process. Who referred you; why they referred you; when can you meet. Prepare your own script because you don't want to just wing it. The voice message is just as important as if you got the person on the line to begin with. One reason people don't get a call back is because they leave bad voice mails.

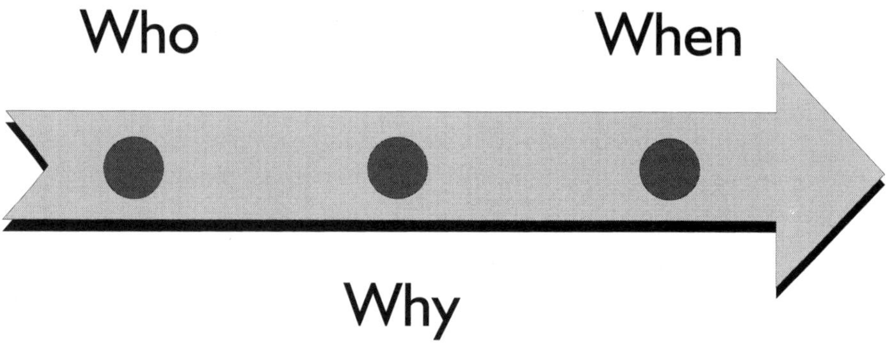

Traits of bad voice mails:

- Too long (my example said slowly is 25 seconds). Anything over 30 seconds is too long.
- Too much information. Keep it to who/why/when.
- Too fast. They don't understand you because you spoke too fast and didn't leave a return number they could understand.
- Too vague. Not enough information is as deadly to a call back as too much information is.
- Too boring. Get away from a monotone voice. Speak as if you were speaking to them at that moment.

You've left the voice mail and now you wait for the call back. Obviously, one of two things happen – they call or they don't. Too many of you give up if they don't call. Here are the next steps if you don't get that return call…

1. One day after leaving the voice mail, send an email (provided you have it) with a cc to your referrer. This has two advantages – the referrer knows you followed through with the referral and will likely give you more and the prospect has a little more pressure to at least respond to you. Depending on the strength of the relationship with the referrer, this by itself could be enough to evoke a call.

2. If there's no call or email reply, then call one day later (48 hours after initial call). If you get voice mail again, here is your script – *"Hi Ms. Jones. This is Dan Weedin from Toro Insurance again. I don't want to haunt you, yet I did promise Jim that I would do my best to meet with you. Would you please call me back at 360-697-1058 (repeat slowly)? I look forward to hearing from you."* Be brief, remind them of the referrer, speak slowly, and repeat your contact information.

3. If there's still no answer two days later, then send a final email to them, again with a cc to your referrer. It should read something like this…

   "Dear Ms. Jones, I regret that we have not been able to connect. We are both busy and I don't want to be a burden. This will be my final attempt to contact you, but feel free to call on me. I would welcome the opportunity to meet with you. Jim Smith says wonderful things about you and I always like meeting interesting people. My contact information is below on my signature line. Best wishes to your continued success.

Then move on. There are only five real reasons that they would not reply in any way to you. They are:

1. The strength of the referral is not as strong as you thought (at least from their point of view).
2. They are legitimately dealing with a business or personal crisis and you are rightly not a priority.
3. They don't view your expertise as a priority for them right now.
4. They are not a buyer (be clear with your referrer on whom you want to gain access to…it MUST be the buyer).
5. You are mired in their SPAM filter and they delete your voice mail.

For whatever reason, if you don't get through and/or are ignored after all of this, it's time to move on. Now may not be the right time. IMPORTANT – Never burn bridges. You never know when the right time might be.

Case Study

In summer of 2012, I was given a referral to the CFO of a 100-person operation that was expert in technical writing for aircraft. I contacted the CFO regarding my strong referral and waited. We did exchange a few short emails, yet at some point he stopped contacting me back. Figuring it was either not a priority or of interest, I sent a nice final email and went on about my business.

Fast forward to April of 2013. I'm sitting on a train in Newark, New Jersey, checking my email and this vaguely familiar name pops up. Turns out "Steve" is now interested after all these months. Their largest buyer was requiring them to supply a crisis and disaster recovery plan, which they didn't have. The burners all of a sudden got moved from back to front quickly! Because of our cordial interchange (and I'm assuming that I stopped haunting him), we were able to quickly develop a relationship that now has progressed over multiple projects – a "win-win-win" situation. You just never know when the right time is for your referred prospect, so be ready when it is.

They call you back. Now what?

Believe it or not, I've been asked that question. They call you back and now what do you do? Most of you are screaming into your book or reading device, "go sell a policy!" While this is true, some ways are better than others to accomplish this coming off a strong referral. Let's look at a few of my "Do's and Dont's."

DON'T attempt to sell over the phone. **DO** make an appointment to meet face to face.

- Selling insurance over the phone on a first call for anything more sophisticated than a BOP is amateurish. This is, and always will be, a relationship business. (You keep reading that don't you? It will be on the test.) Many things can be done over the phone or Internet later. The first meeting needs to be in person.

DON'T gush all over them. **DO** be a peer.

- People don't like to be fawned over. What they do like is a trusted advisor that acts like a peer. In what ways can you ensure you act like a peer? Here are five suggestions from me…

    1. Don't overdo the "*Thanks for your time, I know how terribly busy you are and how wonderful it is that you saw for to give me blah blah blah* " bit. You're time is just as important. Instead say, "*It's great to meet you. I'm looking forward to our discussion.*"
    2. Have an agenda. Pick three things that you want to accomplish in that meeting and tell them up front. Something like this – "*Ms. Jones, I know our time is limited, so I thought it would be best to lay out our agendas first. I have several things I'd like to accomplish at this meeting, and I'm sure you do, too. Let's compare and prioritize to make best use of our time together.*" By having an agenda, you come across as professional, prepared, and respectful. Non-peers just say things like, "*So how about those Seahawks!*"

3. Don't allow them to pawn you off on someone else. If they are the decision maker, you need to be with them because they get the check written. If it is a legitimate request from them to speak to perhaps the operations manager, say something like, *"I'm happy to talk with Jim about how the insurance should be programmed. I do want to make sure that we will be able to circle back together at the end. Insurance is actually a strategic decision and you're the person who makes those important decisions. Can we set a date now to re-connect?"* It takes courage to hold them to grabbing their calendar and doing this, but confident peers work that way together. If they don't want to see you back, they consider you a vendor and you still have work to do!
4. Be contrarian and push back when necessary. I'm not talking about being boorish, but I am suggesting that you be prepared to ask questions like, *"What evidence do you have of that?"* Many times your prospects think they know insurance, yet they don't. YOU are the expert. Be prepared to politely disagree and challenge their thinking.
5. You know you've arrived as a peer when they laugh at your humor and/or share information that they normally wouldn't. So the goal here is to act like you belong, take some chances, and be yourself.

DON'T be in a hurry to sell. **DO** be prepared to build a relationship.

- Just because you were referred into this prospect doesn't mean they are willing to consider doing business with you. They may be solely being kind to the referrer.
- I received a very candid response recently from the CEO of a nationally recognized office furniture manufacturer. He was a referral from a fellow Rotarian. I called him up, he kindly accepted, and we met in his conference room. One of the first questions I often ask is, *"What was it that John said that intrigued you enough to take this meeting with me?"* This is a bold question. You learn a lot about what you can expect moving forward and you sound like a peer. In this case, "Cliff" very honestly said, *"Nothing. I took this meeting as a courtesy to John."* When you hear that, be thankful. That means you have a strong referrer! Now you have to be in a position to shine and move forward.

DON'T leave things open-ended. **DO** create a next step.

- I wonder how many good referrals have died premature deaths because the last words out of an agent's mouth were; *"Call me if you are interested in a quote. So long!"* Let's look at some ways to keep the momentum moving forward...

1. Schedule another meeting...now. If they want to learn more or maybe their renewal is months away, don't just walk out without a next meeting. Pull out whatever you use as a calendar and make them do the same. Say, *"I know we are both busy, so it makes sense to get a meeting on our calendars right now, don't you agree? Can we decide upon a date and time now?"* (As you are pulling out your calendar.) Don't leave with things up in the air. Those situations often end with a whimper and a sigh...and no business!
3. If there is no next meeting because the relationship hasn't made it that far, or they purchase insurance from their brother-in-law, find a way to stay on their radar. Ask if you can add them to your mailing list (you have one, right?). Ask if you can occasionally drop by with information that would be beneficial to them. Get their permission for you to stay in some level of contact.
4. One of my favorite lines when I was an agent came when the prospect said they were tight with their agent and couldn't see leaving. I would just say, *"That's fine, but every team needs a backup quarterback. You never know when something might happen to the starter. May I act as your backup quarterback?"* The offer costs nothing and usually draws a chuckle and affirmation. I unseated many starting quarterbacks who were "entrenched" in their positions!

DON'T Embarrass Your Referrer. **DO** make them a hero.

- Certainly you would never embarrass your referrer intentionally. However it can happen if you're not careful. A great way to avoid any conflict is to advise the referrer that you've made an appointment with their colleague. Ask them if there is anything they need to know or topics you should avoid. If there are any topics that should be avoided, they will tell you.
- Don't gush all over your referrer, either. Acknowledge them; talk about your relationship with them; talk about how your prospect knows them. Put the referrer in a good light so that they will want to send you more!
- Being professional and a peer makes them look like a hero regardless of whether you get the business or not. Never burn bridges, and always give value.

Bottom line

Referrals will lead you to instant and sustainable success. Agents and producers are their own worst enemies because they don't do a good enough job in asking for referrals. I would challenge each of you reading this to gain one new referral a day. One a day will lead to about 20 a month and 250 or so a year. Can you advance your business significantly with that number of highly qualified, warm and fuzzy, and ready to be impressed prospects? I think you can. Now go out and spend your time mining for referrals and digging up gold.

Chapter 7
The Closer

Accelerating the sales cycle and acquiring more clients

At the beginning of my consulting career, I was terrific at setting meetings and making proposals. Meetings and proposals don't cost anything except time. The pure reality of it was that my time (which in and of itself is really valuable) was being spent spinning my wheels. I was still in "insurance agent" mode. The law of large numbers was more than just about risk; it was also about writing new business. This mindset always made me in a hurry. I was in a hurry to meet, in a hurry to quote, and in a hurry to write new business.

It wasn't until I mastered the art of "closing," that my career took off. Closing a deal is more than just sales pitches. It's about strong language and vocabulary skills, great listening skills, successful pre-work, building relationships, and high self-confidence. Ultimately the client must know that you genuinely have their best interests at heart.

What makes a great closer in baseball? As I am writing this chapter, New York Yankees great Mariano Rivera was just toasted by his team, the fans, and the city for his accomplishments as the greatest closer in Major League Baseball history. He is destined to enter the Hall of Fame in his first year of eligibility.

Mariano Rivera was a tremendous closer for *five key reasons:*

1. **Skill set**. Yes, he was an exceptional athlete, but many even better athletes never made it nearly as far because they didn't practice their skill. Rivera was a ceaseless learner and developer of his skill. He never took for granted his prowess and up until his retirement concentrated on improving his pitches and his physical fitness.

2. **Self-confidence**. Nobody succeeded more at his position than Rivera did. However, he wasn't perfect. He blew saves and games for the Yankees every year. However, one bad outing never lingered in his mind. He had the immense self-confidence to step up on the mound the

next day and know in his heart and mind that he was going to succeed. Baseball players call that a "short memory." What it really means is a ridiculously high level of self-confidence.

3. **Work Ethic.** This might piggyback on Skill Set above. His God-given abilities got Rivera only so far. His work ethic in developing those skills requisite to become a legend came from all the hard and lonely work that nobody sees in the weight room and the road.

4. **Endurance.** It seemed like Rivera never got hurt. While I'm sure that isn't true, he was always there and available. Woody Allen once suggested that, "80% of life is just showing up." Rivera always showed up.

5. **Strong team.** For the majority of Rivera's career, his Yankee teams were at a minimum competitive, and at a maximum World Champion caliber. He had a strong supporting cast that put him in a position to save so many games and to back him up on the field. Had he played his entire career with an inferior team, he would never have risen to the heights he did.

So what does all of this have to do with you? Good question. All the characteristics I mention above are the same ones you must have to be a successful "closer" in your own right. I understand you will never step on the mound for a major league baseball team, yet if you want to seal the deal with your prospects, these are all necessary. Allow me to illustrate:

1. **Skill Set.** Your skills are persuasion, influence, language, insurance knowledge, and charisma. You're not born with these; rather they are learned and developed. If you don't want to learn or develop these skills, then you're in the wrong role in the insurance business. Sales isn't for you. If you do want to learn how to enhance them, then you're off to a good start.

2. **Self-confidence.** Insurance sales isn't about rejection as I often hear from people. It's about *resiliency*. The innate ability to bounce back from adversity and rejection. You can't have adequate resiliency unless you have a higher than average level of confidence. Confidence can be achieved and improved, though.

3. **Work ethic.** The best and brightest closers in the insurance business are the hardest workers. When I coached high school basketball, I read

a book written by Duke coach Mike Krzyzewski. He preached that your best players had to be the hardest workers. The same is true for you. While the "work" part might look different than a regular desk job, the results will bear out the success or failure. *Consistent effort* is really the definition of work ethic.

4. **Endurance.** In our business that doesn't mean waiting to be called in out of the bullpen. What it implies is showing up to work every day (and I don't refer necessarily the office). It means spending your days focused on marketing activities that get you in front of buyers (the one requirement of any successful sale), performing your due diligence on preparation for a sales call, being available to answer questions quickly and accurately, and being available for your team.
5. **Strong team.** While you might think this is outside of your control, it's not. A baseball player at any position can change teams through free agency or trade if they are not satisfied with the quality of the team or organization. You can, too. Agency owners need to build a strong team culture, and the closer on this team needs to be a team player, not a lone wolf. There is joint accountability in this deal. In order to increase your percentage of "wins," you must have a team that supports you not only emotionally, but also with work.

Bottom line – if you must "eat what you kill" in this business, you might as well be good at it. Every time Mariano Rivera took to the hill for the Yankees, there were a few certainties. One was that he was absolutely the best person for the job. Second, the likelihood of his succeeding was about 90%. Third, he was going to bring value to the spectators watching him and his team regardless of the outcome. Being the absolute best, having a high degree of success, and bringing immense value over a consistent time will lead you to the same lofty heights in your career as it did for him in his vocation.

It's NOW time – Why expiration dates no longer matter

When I was a kid, I started a somewhat odd (yet normal for a 9-year-old boy) collection. Snake skins. That's right, that white, fragile epidermis that once graced the body of a snake. I was always very attentive about carefully preserving the skin and then mounting them one by one on a hangar in my closet. Yes, in case you're wondering, the same closet where my clothes were kept. I was very proud of that snake skin collection and became quite adept at locating them in the yard and then preserving them with the same circumspection as if it were going to be displayed at the Smithsonian Institute.

At 9 years old, I was at an age that I could (and was expected to) put my clothes away. That meant my mother didn't always go into my closet anymore with as much frequency as she had. So my collection grew for about 3 weeks, accumulating in my closet, until one day my mother decided to check my work. The ensuing scream and call for my immediate presence in my room led me to believe that a snake skin collection being stocked in my room was frowned upon. The snake skins were immediately evicted and my heart temporarily broken.

When I started working on the insurance agency side after my brief experience as a company underwriter, I quickly was taught that insurance sales was at a foundational level all about collecting expiration dates (aka x-dates). I was back to collecting snake skins. I just kept making calls, adding skins, and filling up my closet. The problem was, just like the snake skins in my closet (before my mother found them), they all just sat there gathering dust. For all of those x-dates you collect, they do the same until about 90 days before the renewal and you bring them out to play with. There is a better way.

Make no mistake; there are challenges to moving a client mid-term, especially in the property and casualty world. You often have to deal with issues like:

- Cancellation requests and return premiums
- Broker of record letters
- Firing of incumbent agents
- Lagging issues like claims and endorsements
- Lack of commissions until next renewal
- No sense of urgency by prospect

These are all legitimate arguments. However, the reality is that in today's world of "real time" and "just in time," making a change when it is most needed is worth the trouble.

As an agent, you need to keep in mind one very important rule. The rule is predicated on one main question, *What is best for the client?* If it's not best for the client to move carriers or agents, then they shouldn't. That was always a hard one for me to swallow. As a trained sales person who likes to compete, you think you are always better than the other person. While in the majority of cases, you need to feel that way, there are several that just don't make sense. This might be due to familial ties with the insurance. It might be that the other agent had done some miraculous work during some adversity. It might also be that the carrier had a better program. This should never be about you, but always about the best interest of your prospect.

If it is better for them to be with you as a client, then it's up to you to persuade them on why. If you can do that effectively, then why would you wait for six months for them to become a client just because that's when their renewal date is? Too many things can happen in that time frame to foil your plans.

There is a basic tenet among any type of sales professional. The further away you get from your quote or proposal, the less likely it is that you will earn the business. If you've done all the things we are about to talk about in this chapter, and you have gained agreement that you're the best option for the prospect, write the business. Sign the Broker of Record letter, cancel and rewrite the policy, make it as easy as you can for them, and seal the deal.

When I was in the agency business, I rarely did this. I can honestly tell you I spent more time collecting and then coming back later to quote. While I did have success, I wonder how much more I could have had if I had only used this method. Opportunity knocks only once is a myth. It knocks multiple times. But often it only has the best opportunity to have the door opened once. Stop collecting x-dates to be quoted later, and start working on collecting clients that need you now. Before your mother throws them out of the closet…

Finding the economic buyer through all the gatekeepers

As a new consultant in 2005, the biggest hurdle I had to overcome was to talk to the economic buyer.

> **Definition**: The *Economic Buyer* is the person who has authority to pay you immediately. They can make a check be cut, a credit card to be pulled, or the water to part so the armored cars full of cash can make it in. Importantly, they are also the person whose goals and objectives are the most important. Don't kid yourself, insurance is a strategy item and shouldn't be delegated until after a decision to move is made.

The true economic buyer can range from hard to track down to stealth-like. People in a position of power in an organization are usually adept at delegating things they don't want to do, or shouldn't be doing, to direct reports or underlings. Insurance normally doesn't float to the top of their list because they view it as a commodity. I am going to state that point again (so look for it on your test) – most economic buyers view insurance as a commodity, so deflect it to others to weed out the crowd that wants to sell it to them.

All of you reading this book don't offer insurance to the same target audience. I will offer that every single one of you at some point will deal with a gatekeeper, even if you're on the retail side of the business. Consider this table:

The gatekeeper conundrum

Insurance	**Buyer**	**Gatekeeper**
Commercial	President	Executive Assistant
Health/Benefits	Chief Financial Officer	Human Resources
Personal	Spouse #1	Spouse #2
Workers Compensation	Chief Financial Officer or President	Human Resources or Operations
Large Commercial	CFO	Consultant
All of the above	All of the above	Incumbent agent

** Note that in personal insurance involving life, auto, or home, you need both spouses present to make a decision. One will be the true economic buyer but will potentially defer making a decision if the other one (often an influencer) isn't there.

Many times the issues are more internal than external. The gatekeepers almost always have some stake in the game. They may have a good relationship with the incumbent agent and don't want to rock the boat. They may be the one tasked with all of the work in a transition and don't want to add it to their already full plate. They may fear being rebuked by their boss if they let a slippery insurance agent through the gate. In addition, you must consider the incumbent agent an internal source of "gatekeeping." When I was an agent, many of my clients that were approached by other agents would "delegate" the review of agent and company to me. In fact, that practice was what eventually led me into consulting, as too often I had to tell my clients quite candidly that the other market was better than what I could get!

Important – you should be putting yourself in this most trusted advisor role. You should be the one delegated the duty of being gatekeeper for the insurance. How do you do this? Simple. You tell your client. Use language like this…

"Joan, I'm not the repository of all insurance information. I'm certain you will have other agents want to quote your insurance. I have no issues with that, in fact that's how I earned your business. All I ask is that you provide me the opportunity to review any proposals, quotes, or programs prior to making a final decision. I promise you will get my honest report and recommendation for what is in your best interests."

I know this is counterintuitive and may go against everything you were ever taught, but hear me out on this because I was (and often still am) the gatekeeper for my clients in my role as their consultant. Agents that shy away from and avoid conversations on competition are viewed as commodities. Agents with enough confidence in themselves and their markets, *AND those that put their client's best interest first*, are viewed as trusted advisors and will never lose an account because they were blindsided or not given an opportunity to scrutinize the competition.

Getting to the economic buyer as quickly as possible is your number one goal in prospecting. Don't waste your time sending proposals to someone who can say "NO," and can't say, "YES." You should only offer proposals to economic buyers, and you should build that trusted advisor relationship with them, not the gatekeeper.

IMPORTANT: Gatekeepers are not bad people. They are not the enemy. I poke a little fun in the next section about getting past the gatekeeper to your ultimate decision maker, but make no mistake – gatekeepers must be treated well. They are usually in that position because they have gained a large amount of equity with their boss for their ability to do their job. If you view them as your enemy, your road will be more difficult. If you view them as a potential ally, you will increase the likelihood of success exponentially.

There are many theories and approaches out there floating around cyberspace and bookstores. Allow me to throw mine out for your consideration.

Dan's 9 Strategies for Blowing Up the Gatekeeper Without Leaving a Mark

1. **Do your homework**

   As we discussed in marketing, doing your homework has never been easier with the Internet. It will only get easier in the future. This is a simple identification process. Find out who is in charge of the budget for insurance. That's your economic buyer.

2. **Be prepared**

   The Boy Scouts know what they are talking about! Being prepared here means understanding that you may run into a gatekeeper. Finding one at any level or type of insurance should not come as a shock to you and leave you flailing about for your next words. Go into every situation expecting someone to block your clean path to the buyer.

3. **Practice your language**

   Part of being prepared means having your words ready to say with confidence and purpose. The best, and I mean BEST way to practice is with role-playing. Role-playing may not sound like much fun, and my guess is many may not like it because they have been caught looking foolish a time or two. Better to look foolish with your peers than with a gatekeeper.

4. **Avoid the Eddie Haskell Scheme**

   Some of you may be too young to remember the classic 1960s television series, *Leave it to Beaver*. In the show, one of the characters was a duplicitous teenage boy named Eddie Haskell (portrayed brilliantly by Ken Osmond). When with his friends he was scheming, conniving, and mischievous; when with his parents, he was unctuous to the point of being sickening.

   You need to treat the gatekeeper with the respect their position in the organization (or the family) demands, but being obsequious to any degree is never good. Gatekeepers (just like Ward and June Cleaver in the show) will see right through veiled gratitude, gushiness, and fawning.

Don't think I overstate this because I've seen it. If I were to be truly candid, I may have crossed the line unintentionally myself when I was an agent. It's easier to do than you think. Even the best and the brightest, in an effort to win favor and get to the "next level," will slip into ingratiating language and behavior. Just be careful.

5 **John sent me...**

It's always better to come warm rather than cold. Referrals and recommendations are always to your advantage, especially if the gatekeeper is also familiar with and likes the recommender. The referral can come in the form of a name being used with permission, or an endorsement from an association or group.

When I was a commercial agent, my main company carrier was Federated Mutual Insurance. Federated had a strategic marketing plan that was based around association and buying group recommendations. At the time, they had obtained strong endorsements from groups like NAPA and other state and local associations. I would collect reference and introduction letters from all of these associations and call on members. To me this isn't cold calling because I have a warm introduction by someone they know. This kind of influence often prompts a gatekeeper to make an introduction with the buyer.

6. **Relish objections**

You might as well because you're going to get them. Later in this chapter, I will arm you with language to use. Just know for right now, that if you aren't ready for an immediate objection, you're being negligent.

7. **WIIFM**

You need to convey to the gatekeeper that it's in their best interest to allow you an audience with the buyer. We all think at some of level of WIIFM (What's in it for me). Gatekeepers do, too. The truth is that it is in their best interest because you have something of great value to share. Just make sure you know what that value is!

8. **The end around**

If the gatekeeper is resolute in keeping you at bay, then you might have to run an "end around." In American football, the end around is an offensive play used to score a touchdown (or at least gain big yardage).

Teams that have fast players use big and fast blockers to run around the defensive players, using their speed and agility. In order to be successful, the team running the end around needs to have fast players.

You might need to be fast, too. If you can't get in by force (running up the middle), then you might dash around the end and outrun the gatekeeper! Some ways to get directly to the buyer without the assistance of his assistant include:

- Locating his or her direct line and calling. These aren't so hard to get anymore. In fact, many buyers stick it right on their business card.
- Join associations or groups that the buyer belongs to and get introduced (e.g. Rotary, trade groups, charitable organizations).
- Attend functions that you know they will be at. Find a professional way to be introduced and ask to schedule a meeting.
- Find a common friend through any of your social media platforms. LinkedIn will probably be the best.

9. **Blow them up**

This may take you to an uncomfortable place. You should never be rude, aggressive, or mean. But the reality is that unless you meet with the economic buyer, you will never get this business. It's better to know now than waste years beating your head up against the gate.

You don't need any C4 in this case. Explosives just don't leave a good lasting impression and they will leave a mark. What you will need to do is run an end around to find the buyer. Tell them in a very skilled manner that your attempts to reach them with very important information have been thwarted. You are not there to be vengeful, but feel it's in the buyer's best interest to know.

Stop using insurance as a weapon

Understand this important concept and you will be 50% ahead of your competitors (unless they are also reading this book). The concept revolves around insurance agents' incessant desire to use insurance and all the jargon and gibberish associated with this industry as a weapon.

This is what I mean: 90% of the agents I have worked with since becoming a consultant for the buyer spend an inordinate amount of time talking insurance.

Your buyer doesn't want to talk insurance; you've basically talked them into doing it. What they do know is that they need to purchase it. It might be required (car, home, health, multiple liability polices) or a priority (life, business, disability). Regardless, they don't speak the insurance language, nor will ever use it while traveling so don't use it with them.

My five tactics for removing insurance as a sharp object are pretty simple and actually should make you happier. If you commit to changing your paradigm and going down a more manageable path, you will gain more clients by sealing the deal more often.

1. **Remove ALL acronyms from your proposal, quote and language.** No more ITV (insurance to value), RC (replacement cost), ACV (actual cash value), IBNR (incurred but not reported), BI (business income), D & O (directors and officers), EPL (employment practices liability), or PAP (personal auto policy). I promise you that I've read proposals and quotes that bear these and other acronyms that the agent has to explain. Make this your rule of thumb – dump the acronyms and write all the words out.

> *Note*: I read on AllAcronyms.com that there are 1,033 insurance industry acronyms. Can you imagine the poor sap that had to go through all of those?

2. **Stop leading off with name, rank, and serial number.** Tell me if this sounds familiar. Proposal starts with the prospect's name (and maybe a blurry photo of their building for commercial), followed by pages of information about the agency, its history in the community, all the team members with mini-biographies, some legal disclaimer that this isn't the real policy; and finally pages of coverages, exclusions, and numbers, ending with a list of premium options at the end.

   Your clients are already confused enough about insurance, especially if you're dealing with personal or small business insurance. Larger organizations and companies are more sophisticated, but they will get bored quickly.

   Your proposal needs to focus on them and how they are better served by putting their business with you. The proposal should be the culmination of a process where you've reached a conceptual agreement to work together and now the question is "how," not "if." Focus on their objectives for insurance, not the methodology behind it. Methodology is the policy limits, coverages, exclusions, and fancy language. Yes, these are ultimately important to be accurate but the real reason they are purchasing the insurance should be foremost in their minds, so remind them.

Examples of Objectives

- *Personal insurance* – Sustainable and long-term lifestyle protection.
- Commercial insurance – Assurance that speedy recovery of assets will minimize the length and impact of any disaster.
- *Life* – The beneficiaries will have full peace of mind that finances will not become a burden.
- *Group Medical* – That employees will be happy with the service and benefits they receive. (Note – my clients have always been concerned about cost, yet the happiness of their employees has always been the priority. Always.)
- *Long-term Care* – The family will never have a financial burden to bear in the event of an assisted living situation.

If the focus is on personal and business outcomes, and the limits are correct and adequate, then premium is diminished as an objection.

3. **Include more definitions.** It's okay to include definitions of coverages, exclusions, and other tricky insurance stuff. They know they aren't insurance experts. They may need to look over your proposal later and forgot what you told them. How cool would it be for them if they had a definition of coinsurance and an example of what it does? Don't think that you'll insult them. Make it easier for them to understand.

4. **List all your markets quoted.** If you're not a captive agent, then you've probably quoted several markets for your prospect. Don't be shy to show them your work. It means that you did your due diligence, and then put an explanation as to why you are making your recommendation.

5. **Stop using company-produced templates.** Everyone I've ever seen looks like it has come out of *Excel Hell*. Rows and rows of formatted numbers and words that make no sense. It makes your prospects dizzy. Simple is always the better option.

The power of language

You have read that I frequently reference my professional mentor, Alan Weiss. That's because I've been working closely with him for many years and some of it actually rubbed off on me. I believe the same will go for you. Here is another one. Alan has a theory that goes:

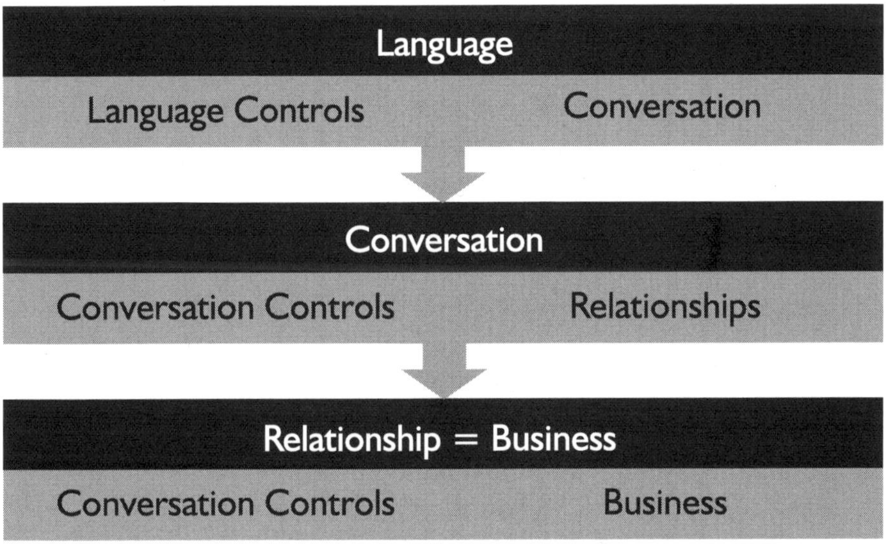

This section will provide you with language you can use with the situations detailed above in my nine strategies. Please understand that the majority of these options are geared towards a business insurance situation. If you're in personal lines or benefits, feel free to manipulate certain words to make the language work for you!

Identifying the buyer

- Who controls the resources required to purchase the insurance?
- Who has initiated the request for proposal?
- Who will accept or reject proposals?
- Do you have to seek anyone else's approval?
- If you and I were to shake hands, could we begin today?

Establishing objectives (see above)

- Why are you seeking quotes from other agents? (You might be surprised.)
- How are you going to define your Return on Investment?
- What do you most want to accomplish with your insurance?
- What is the issue you're trying to resolve?
- What's your biggest priority and why?

Establishing metrics

- How will we know we've accomplished your intent?
- How will you measure my value to you?
- How would you know it if you tripped over it? (My personal favorite.)

Assessing value

- How will working with me (our agency) improve your current situation?
- How will you personally be better supported?
- What is the intangible impact to your organization (or family)?
- How will our results impact your bottom line?
- How will our results impact your peace of mind?

Preventing the unforeseen

- Is there anything we haven't discussed that can get in the way of us working together?
- What do you estimate the probability is of our going forward?
- At this point, are you still going to make the decision yourself?
- Are you awaiting any other proposals or quotes?

Overcoming objections

There are really only four classifications of objections. All objections you will hear fall under one of these classes:

No Time | No Need

No Money | No Trust

I don't care what you've heard before as far as a reason to stall progress or simply say no, but I promise you that one of these is the root cause to rejection. And as you will see, three of the reasons are specious and only one has any validity. The good news is that you control that one.

> *Note*: Objections are not always bad. They most always mean opportunity. If someone needs clarification, a better understanding of a concept, or desires examples and case studies, then that means they are interested. You can tell the objections that are meant to increase clarity and those used to usher you out the door ("Boy, look at the time!"). Relish objections that offer you real opportunity. Learn how to overcome objections that are based in lack of relationship.

No time

Time is not a resource issue. We all have the same amount of it. It's a priority issue. They have time; they're just not giving it to you! The "no time" objection is really saying, "I'm not interested, leave me alone." You have to become an ***object of interest*** and ***create a desire*** to hear more from you. Here are a few tactics (and language) you can use to overcome this objection:

- "Mr. Buyer, I agree we all have to maximize how we spend our time. I would never want to waste yours. If I can quickly show you a way to assure that your children will all be able to attend college without financial burden, would you be interested?"
- "Ms. Buyer, time is always a factor for all of us, including me. That's why I would never waste yours. If I can show you a way to enhance your peace of mind and potentially save money at the same time, would you be willing to invest 30 minutes?"
- Ask your prospect if they would agree be added to your monthly mailing list. By providing provocative, contrarian, and edgy information, you will over time be more likely to create interest.
- Logic makes people think; emotion makes them buy. You need to create emotion to get them to invest their time.
- Be bold. Ask what is missing. "Mr. Buyer, I've obviously not shown you the value of meeting with me. What did I say, or not say, that doesn't provide you with the impetus to invest 30 minutes with me?" There is no reason not to be bold. At this point, they aren't buying from you anyway!

No need

For some of you, this is not a product objection. If you sell homeowners, car, business, group medical, and workers compensation insurance, they need it (whether they like it or not). Their objection will be that they don't need YOU! This can often be the brother-in-law agent, the agent they've been with since the beginning of time, or the association agent (USAA, John Deere, etc.).

For others of you in the life, disability, long-term care, and consulting field, they actually don't "need" you as your product is not required by law or contract.

It's up to you to create a need in either case.

- "Why do you feel that you don't need this protection?" (Get to the true cause.)
- "What evidence do you have that you don't need it?" (Challenge their assumptions.)
- Bring up case studies, examples, personal stories, and current events as illustrations of why they need it. But here is the kicker. You need to take those lessons and compare them in metaphor form to their lives. Otherwise, they draw no distinction to how it helps them. This would be akin to trying to draw a parallel for life insurance between a 25-year

old man with no wife or children and a 50-year old man with a wife and three kids going to college. The 25-year old just can't grasp it. You need to connect the dots.

Connecting the Dots: I was out walking my dog around the neighborhood when a little floppy-eared dog came charging out at us. It was readily apparent from his big smile that he wanted to be friends. My dog Bella was unimpressed and annoyed. I kept trying to shoo him away to make him go back home, but he had a little crush on Bella and ended up following us all the way back to my house. I had to dump Bella back inside and walk him back and find where he came from. Luckily with a little help from one of the neighbors, we found his home (about a quarter mile away) and I returned him. But that's not the end of the story.

After grabbing a quick bite of lunch, I decided to go back out and take Captain Jack for his walk before I headed back to work. We had just turned the corner of our driveway when we saw the same little dog running like scalded cat back towards my house! I knew Captain Jack was going to have none of this little guy, so I quickly deposited Jack back in the house and made the same déjà vu trek back to the house!

The owner was befuddled. She couldn't figure out how this little ragamuffin kept escaping. Then I saw it. Their fence had an opening in it. Not big enough for a German Shepherd, but easily big enough for this squirt.

Transition into Metaphor: Many of us think we are protected by our own "fence." In our case, the fence is our insurance policy. While originally it might have been just fine, time and circumstances change. When these people first had their home, the fence was fine. When they added a diminutive dog to their yard, it's not so good anymore. As you add to your life, the hole in your insurance "fence" creates gaps in your protection. Not having it regularly looked at by someone NOT your neighbor may be worth your time investment.

Personal stories as a metaphor work really well in creating need. Why? Because you're taking something that your prospect can wrap their head around and then give them a new way of thinking about their situation. The very best closers are the ones that can weave a personal story into a powerful need.

No money

This might be the oldest objection on record dating back to the oldest professions in the world! Just like time, money is not a resource issue. Again, it's a priority issue. My assumption is that the prospect you're talking has the lights on, machines running, mortgage or rent up to date, and employees paid. I'm not staying their priorities are wrong. They are not. You just aren't a priority to give money to.

In the money objection, most often it's a comparative thing. You're either more costly, or not enough of a bargain to make a switch in their minds. Or, if your product is not required (life or disability insurance), they aren't motivated enough to cut something else out to finance the protection.

Here are some ideas on overcoming this objection:

- "But isn't that exactly why you need me?" (A reversal approach. If they are really that broke, a crisis might be fatal to their future.)
- "If I can demonstrate a substantial return on your financial investment, would you be willing to reconsider?" (Sometimes you need to validate ROI.)
- Establish that your program, policy, project, and you have a greater ROI than what they currently have. This is based on value. Value always trumps price. If it didn't you wouldn't see any Mercedes Benz, Cartier watches, or Roberto Cavalli jeans ($2,000 in 2013). There are much more inexpensive cars, watches, and trousers out there that serve the same purpose. The name of the game is value, prestige, and priority.
- "What can we do to overcome that?" (Demonstrate joint accountability.)
- "What are your priorities?"

No trust

This is the real one. In fact, all of the others really stem from lacking trust. I don't have to remind you that in significant matters, people do business with those that they trust. If you have not gained that level of credibility yet, then you'll not sell them a policy. To add to that, if you did sell them a policy without gaining all their trust, it was done on a "price-only" basis and you're a commodity.

The biggest source of all failure in adequately reaching a trusting relationship is that insurance agents and brokers all too often try to rush the *relationship cycle*. You can refer to it as a sales cycle if you want, but truly it's a *relationship cycle*.

My relationship cycle as a consultant is no different really than yours as an agent. In fact, it might be a bit harder seeing that I'm not a necessity and it could be harder to explain what value I bring to the table. I was referred to a new prospect and based on the strength of that referral garnered a meeting. But it wasn't that easy to get. "Brian" was willing to grant me 30 minutes and no more. He valued the referrer's opinion and for that reason only was willing to invest a small amount of time. I knew that I had to quickly gain his trust to even hope for a second meeting.

When I walked in to his office, he was very congenial. We actually began a conversation about an interesting object he had in his office. We talked about 10 minutes and I was prepared to shorten my discussion in the interest of building trust. To my surprise, at the end of the brief conversation Brian looked at me, smiled, and said, "Okay, your 30 minutes start now. I won't count that against you. That was for fun." He was testing whether he actually liked me. We then continued on discussing his business, his concerns, and my work with companies similar to his. As we came to the end of our time (we exceeded 30 minutes, but on his inclination, not mine), Brian offered, "This has been valuable for me. I think there is an opportunity to work together. We should set up another meeting and I will include a couple of my key people. Is that all right with you?" Uh…let me think about that. YES!

In about a one-hour time frame, I had taken a relationship that was barely warm, into one that had a sense of purpose and trust. You can do that as well, but you have to follow some guidelines.

Dan's 8 Simple Rules to Gaining Trust in 60 Minutes or Less

1. **Do your homework.** You've seen this before in the marketing section. Invest time in learning about the business, the individual, or the organization you're about to talk to. Even if you work in the personal lines arena, a quick search engine inquiry may bring up information that is helpful.

2. **Ask questions and listen.** You're not a trained seal. Dog and pony shows do very little to engender trust. Ask good questions (it's okay to

use notes) and then shut up and listen. When you get that little urge to interrupt and inject something, squash it! Make observations and ask follow-up questions.

3. **Stay in the moment.** Don't start thinking of your next retort while he or she is still talking. You might miss something important. Be attentive and be ready to respond based on what was just said. Note – pausing for a several seconds after the prospect finishes speaking won't make you internally combust. It makes you look thoughtful and unrehearsed.

4. **Use stories.** You may be asked about your experience and how you've helped others. The best way to illustrate this is with a story. Have a few prepared *before* you walk into the office. Learn how to most effectively tell stories so that they create interest. Stories are the best tool to help your prospect understand how you might work together to their benefit.

5. **Don't pitch.** Rather be the catcher. Crummy sales people pitch out of the gate. Great relationship builders seek to "catch" information that will help them develop a long-term relationship, rather than a short-term customer. Prospects can smell "pitchers" as soon as they walk in the office.

6. **Arrive on time.** I'm always baffled when agents show up late to a meeting. It's a terrible way to start. I plan on being there 10 minutes early in the parking lot; gather everything (including my thoughts) together; and walk in 5 minutes prior.

   Sometimes things happen (traffic, car problems, etc.) that are outside of your control. You can easily pull over (or better yet use a hands free device) to call and explain the situation. If they don't have a commitment after, it shouldn't be a problem. If they have a "hard stop," then being late and reducing your time is probably not in your best interest. It would be better to re-schedule and start from scratch.

Golfers are creatures of routine. Watch a professional golfer who is preparing to putt on the green. If they are distracted for some reason, they don't do what amateurs do. Amateurs like me stand over the ball, wait until the distraction is over, and then miss the putt. Professionals walk away from the ball and begin their pre-putt routine all over again. Then they walk up to the ball just like the distraction never happened and sink the putt.

When thrown off of our routine in preparation for any meeting (much less a new prospect), amateurs will try to cram 45 minutes into 25 minutes just for the hope of seeing the prospect. The result is the same as a missed putt, except here it's a missed opportunity. The meeting is rushed and the prospect is unimpressed. It's better to re-start the process and re-schedule and make a good impression.

7. **Stay on time.** Determine before how much time you have. It's a simple question – "Jane, in an effort to maximize our time together, how long are you able to give our meeting?" During the meeting, make sure you are keeping track of time. If they offer to extend that time, fine. That means you're doing something right. Or, they may have an obligation after and you being punctual shows professionalism. You can always end a meeting by scheduling the next one before you walk out the door.
8. **Offer value.** It's okay to give away a little free advice. It's okay to challenge assumptions and ask hard questions. It's okay to make them think. You want your prospect to consider in their head, "Gee, if I get this much value and I'm not even a client, I wonder what I would get if I were?"

Here's your sign

There are a few easy ways to tell if you're gaining trust with your prospect. If you're not seeing these yet, your relationship is not strong enough to earn their business. Identify them and you know you're on your way.

- The prospect shares business information (confidential, proprietary, or just even internal) with you, as if you were their agent.
- They demonstrate humor. They enjoy your humor and offer banter themselves.
- They lean forward. This is Body Language 101. It means they are interested in what they are hearing.

- They ask questions. People who are bored or uninterested are trying to shorten the conversation, not lengthen it.
- They share personal information on their family, pets, and hobbies.
- They respect your challenges. This is a big one. Your prospects are not looking for assenters. They want advisors to challenge them.
- They see you as a peer, not a vendor. If they are willing to hear a different opinion, willing to laugh, ask a lot of questions, and share information, then you are considered a peer. That is the position you are working to attain BEFORE trying to sell them a policy.

Once you've gained trust and conceptual agreement on a path to follow for whatever insurance you are recommending, sealing the deal should be easy. Without trust, you will only be a mediocre closer. You will be inconsistent, often disappointed, and much too frequently pressing. If you are expert in building genuine, solid relationships first, then you will find that your closing ratio significantly increases and you're having more fun.

Chapter 8

The Holy Grail

Recruiting and retaining talent in a new age of insurance

My first real job out of college was in the insurance business. I was first hired at United Pacific Insurance Company near Seattle in August 1989. You might say that like many of you, I "accidentally" slipped into the business and never left!

I had walked for my graduation in June, but needed two more classes in the summer to officially graduate. I was newly married and looking for a job. As a History major that originally wanted to teach and coach basketball, and now had changed my mind, I was desperate for options!

My wife Barb had taken a job as a receptionist at a boutique insurance agency off the shores of Lake Union in downtown Seattle shortly after we were married. I was still in school and somebody had to make some money! We only had one car, so she would drive me to the campus at the University of Washington and then drive about five miles to work. After I was done with classes and my on-campus job, I would hop the bus to where she worked and pick up her and the car. I got an opportunity to meet and talk with some of the agents and staff members there. I realized insurance was more than I had thought it was, and based on some of their lifestyles, I figured it made really good money! One of the agents, named Chuck, was very supportive. He was in his early 40s and laid out a picture of what a career in insurance might look like. When I got an opportunity to interview at United Pacific, he encouraged me as an opportunity to learn the business and see where it would take me. I heeded his advice.

I got the job as a personal lines underwriter. Ironically, a guy I went to high school with landed the other personal lines underwriter position in the same unit. It was a great situation for me. It paid a whopping $20,000 a year starting salary. In 1987, I thought I'd hit the jackpot! I was just married with no kids and money burning a hole in my pocket!

I quickly learned that insurance, like any other business, could be volatile. Three days into my new job, we were all informed that our sister company out of Philadelphia, Reliance Insurance Company, had "merged' with us. This would be a "good thing" for us as a company and as employees. My pal and fellow underwriter Brian and I were pretty naïve at that time and went along with it. Looking back, I remember some of the crestfallen and scared faces of our more veteran co-workers. They knew what was eventually going to happen.

Over the course of the next 12 months, many older employees lost their jobs. There was one major motivating factor, outside of money, as to why that happened. In the late 1980s, technology was beginning to hit its unstoppable stride. In college I had started working with computers, so I was more than capable. My co-workers in their 50s and older weren't so good. They had trouble using computers, were slow, and in many cases obstinate about trying. Some were selected out and some "self-selected" out as the "merger" turned into an acquisition. The younger members, like Brian and me, kept our jobs. While cost was definitely a portion of that decision, there is no doubt the capabilities we had with technology, the ability we had to continue to grow with it, and the brightest future opportunity for the company, came through us.

I ended up leaving a year later as I realized underwriting and my personality weren't really congruent. I made the leap over to one of my insurance agency clients to become a personal lines producer. Like United Pacific and Reliance, my new agency was drawn to hiring young talent to perpetuate and build for the future.

The job with Bell-Anderson Insurance wasn't necessarily easy to get. I did know them and they knew me, which is always a good start. They put me through a written caliper test, which confirmed my aptitude for sales over desk jockeying. After a few interviews with the big bosses, I was hired. I was sent off to a satellite office in a neighboring town that boasted all of one employee. I was given a desk, a thick rate book with small print and hundreds of pages, and a hearty "Go get 'em kid!" And off I went.

My situation may not be too unlike many of you over the age of 45. The times and technology dictated a lot of that. However, my personal motivating factor was to get a job that would give me the opportunity to create the lifestyle I wanted for my now growing family and me. Like most of us at that time, we took a job, didn't expect much training, and learned from the school of hard knocks. If it took time to learn and we had to endure bad bosses, poor work environments, and crummy pay to start, so be it.

Note: To be very clear, I had none of those three issues at Bell-Anderson. I had great and supportive bosses, excellent work environments and co-workers, and fair compensation. I left eventually for reasons outside of them that included a wild hair and dreams of entrepreneurship.

So what's wrong with this picture? Nothing in 1989. Today, it may be the recipe for hiring poor employees, hiring good employees that leave you for greener and richer pastures, and potentially damaging experiences for your revenue, clients, culture, and reputation.

Who are you looking for?

Just like good college football coaches, you'd better know what positions you need for your team. Whenever I talk to groups about "talent," the natural tendency is to gravitate towards sales. That would be a mistake.

Defining Talent: Talented people are looking for jobs. They are not all necessarily "young." Many are coming out of military careers or have been laid off from other jobs due to the economy and looking for a fresh start. I hesitate to always call talent "young" because I'm of the opinion that if someone is intelligent, skilled, and coachable, they should be able to be a star for you.

I've created a short list to help you determine the skills you need in your agency. I'm certain that people reading this book will have insurance agencies that range from two to 2,000 employees. Size doesn't matter so much as does what happens in the day-to-day operations of your agency. My experience is that most offices operate as a small business. Even the national brokers keep office counts fairly modest so as to be most efficient and client friendly.

The skill set

- **Leaders** – Leaders do the right things. They are visionary. They are communicators. They are inspirational. People are willing to run through brick walls for them. And they are hard to find. The leader of an agency is normally *The Boss*. *The Boss* gained his or her right to lead much like royalty in Great Britain did...they were born into it, or they had the money to buy it. Neither case ensures that a leader is in the house. Many agencies falter because *The Boss* isn't a good leader, but rather an excellent sales person. That means *The Boss* may need to find a hired gun* to lead, or learn how to become a leader himself. A leader deals with management issues, culture, discipline, and strategy. It takes time away from producing new business. If you want to be both the leader and a producer, you have a tall order in front of you. Make sure you are doing the right things to enhance your agency, rather than those things that detract. As you can imagine, the dominoes fall from here!

> **Definition** – *A Hired Gun* is a person who has the specific skill set that is most needed by a company. They didn't found the agency, they are not family, they may not even have stock options. What they do is make sure that their skills are going to dramatically enhance the business. CEOs are often hired guns brought on by the board of directors (which might include the founder, the principal shareholder, etc.) A hired gun may also be a specialist in technology or other area of concern.

- **Managers** – Managers do things right. Notice the difference with leaders. This is not to imply that managers don't do the right things (see Leaders). Managers tend to not be visionaries, but assiduous rule followers and doers. Once given direction, managers excel in guiding and cajoling great efficiency and results from teams. One of the errors that many businesses make is that when growth happens, people that shine in one role (e.g. producer) are "promoted" to a managerial job (e.g. sales manager) that they lack the skills for. Managers are there to do what the name implies... manage. It takes an individual who is detail-oriented, motivated by a job well done, and feeds on results. Example – your sales manager should not be your rock star producer. Michael Jordan was arguably the greatest basketball player ever, yet he couldn't coach. It's the same principle.
- **Producers** – You need people who have a skill set of selling insurance. In the end, you're a sales organization, so this is critical.
- **Service People** – You need people who are skilled in advancing customer relationships and experience. This is NOT the producer. You need a

support staff that is diligent in getting requests for changes done, attentive to the needs of the client, and skilled at rounding out accounts and making referrals. I fear that agencies will hire for this position with less weight to its decision because it's assumed that anyone can do this. Let's be serious, your support staff is the life-blood of your agency. The producers pump in the blood; the support staff keep you from bleeding out! This should be a position that is given great thought and attention when filling.

- **Technology Expert** – One position on your staff needs to be allocated to a person who can ensure you are able to even answer the phone. Everything that happens in a typical insurance agency requires some level of technical expertise. And I promise you, a week will not go by without at least one technical crisis. This person is critical to your success and needs NO insurance knowledge, training or licensing. If you're in a situation that you can't afford one in-house (if you have more than 10 employees, hire an in-house), then get yourself a "hired gun." In this case, a hired gun may be an outside consultant.
- **Social Media Expert** - Yes, you read that correctly. You read in a previous chapter the importance of social media for any size of agency. I think this position screams to hire a college or high school intern. You don't need to train them in insurance. They can help you get out what you need to your audience in cyberspace more effectively and efficiently. And, a bonus will be that you're showing them a side of the industry that they never would have otherwise seen. That's what originally happened to me. You might have a future technology guru working for you!
- **Receptionist** – This position has been taken for granted and almost made irrelevant by many agencies. How do I know? I've seen it first hand.

  Here is what happens if you're a smaller agency, the CSR absorbs the position. Now in addition to doing their first job, they get to be interrupted and distracted by a ringing phone. You might have a CSR who is well trained in communications and charisma, yet the additional burden means neither job gets done well and leads to anxiety or apathy.

  OR…you decide that an automated system works. Ugh.

  One of the areas I've seen larger brokers and agencies excel in is the receptionist position. One of my clients is a national broker and has a metropolitan downtown office. They employ two receptionists up front to greet and answer phones. These two people are exceptional. They are friendly, never hurried, remember your name, and always offer you a beverage. This particular client has done well in hiring a good face for the agency.

Here is the bad news for you smaller agencies. These large downtown office style agents rarely get walk-ins. The walk-ins they get normally pushed the wrong floor number on the elevator. They get company underwriters, marketing professionals, and yahoos like me.

> *Definition of a "yahoo*: Unsophisticated person. Synonyms include – boor, clod, clodhopper, clodpoll, buffoon, hayseed, lout, lummox (my personal favorite), oaf, and rube. A great term when using self-deprecating humor.

Small agencies get more traffic yet have reduced the role of the face of their agency. The result is that you look, feel, and smell like a commodity. If you have the lowest price, you might get the business. That's NOT what you want to portray. Hire a good, friendly, and charismatic receptionist, even if it's part-time during your busiest periods. It will be worth the investment.

Bottom line – these people all are critical for your success. These are all skilled positions that require specific roles and responsibilities, training, and mentoring. To rise above your competition and be distinct or breakthrough, you need to have these roles filled and carried out by talented people. How would you rate yourself on these roles right now? What do you need to do to elevate?

From the BLOG

Yesterday, my daughter Kelli called with an emergency. Her 1997 Nissan Sentra (Yes, that's right it's 16-years-old. We're lucky it still moves.) was in the shop to get new breaks. Turns out that the frame was starting to get rusted and was in danger of falling off if someone sneezed too hard. This took the final bill to a little over what she was prepared to deal with. Being a good father that wants to see his child remain safe while driving an old jalopy, I offered to take care of the rest. Unfortunately, her call came at 6:15 in the morning (she lives on the East Coast) and I was in no position to pay at that time.

I rolled out of bed, grabbed a cup of coffee and some pancakes (priorities) and went into my office to call the shop (which is a national "brand-name" establishment). Kelli had sent me a text with the phone number, so I dialed it from there. Here was the response I heard – *"This call is unable to be completed at this time. Please try again."* I looked at my phone somewhat dumbstruck because I knew I couldn't have dialed incorrectly. I tried again with the same response. I then tried on my landline thinking that somehow this might attain a different result (remember it's about 6:45 by now).

"This call is unable to be completed at this time. Please try again."

So now I'm sure that Kelli has sent me the wrong phone number, so I text her with my air of indignation. She told me the number was correct, and that all the workers were in the shop. Nobody was there to answer the phone. Really? You're in a competitive business and potential customers are greeted with *"This call is unable to be completed at this time. Please try again,"* instead of a voice mail? That's crazy.

I'm pretty sure that you don't run your insurance agency that way. I'm certain you have some type of electronic voice mail or answering service. However, how strong is your ability to take in calls from clients and prospects? Try answering these five questions…

- Does a real live person answer your phone during business hours always? I mean, always? Don't tell me you can't do it because they did it in the 1950s just fine. I am constantly amazed at how many insurance agents (and I call a lot of them) are fine with an electronic greeting over a real person. Here is the simple answer…hire a really talented and cheerful receptionist and then have at least one backup in case she or he is on the phone. That backup should also at least sound pleasant on the phone. Having a tertiary backup isn't unreasonable in this technological age. I guarantee you your clients and prospects want to talk to a human when they call.
- Do you make your callers go through electronic hell in order to talk to someone? You know what I mean…you go through the nine circles of suffering (à la Dante's *Inferno* in his 14th century poem *Divine Comedy*) jabbing at numbers and trying to remember what number was associated with whom.
- If you do have a real person answer, do they sound like they want to be there? Okay, stop laughing. I know you are recalling one of those

"conversations." The doorman at a luxury hotel is the most important person at that hotel because they set the tone of the visit. Your receptionist is the most important person in that office because they set the tone of your client and prospect experience. Make sure you take as much effort in hiring a good receptionist as you do in buying that $300 coffee maker.

- How customer friendly is your entrance and waiting area? Is it inviting and warm, or does it show everyone working and talking on the phone? Do you offer complimentary coffee, tea, and water or do they have to fend for themselves? Would you feel welcome walking into your own agency?
- Voice mail is fine. I use it all the time as I am a company of one (Captain Jack refuses to answer the phone). But I've heard voice mails from goofy to confusing. You don't need to leave a 45-second voice mail telling them your life history. You also want something more than 'Leave a message." The whole point of voice mail is to make leaving that message easy. Here's all you need – your name (*Hi, this is Dan Weedin*), the ask (*please leave your name and phone number*), the commitment (*and I will call you back within 90 minutes*). I understand you feel compelled to leave that goofy language that coverage can't be bound. Do it quickly (*I can't bind coverage with email so don't even try it*). Using a little humor never hurts.

You may have noted I said I would call you back in 90 minutes. That's my standard and I commit to it. Saying "I will call you back as soon as possible" is really just weak. That could mean three days or maybe never. We live in an instant gratification world. You have constant access to your voice mail. How hard is it to commit to a standard of calling people back? The reality is that people are scared they can't deliver. If I can, you can. It's a matter of discipline and courtesy.

So while you may have chuckled a little over my experience with the repair shop, don't get too comfortable. You may want to audit your own agency's practices and see how user-friendly you are…or aren't!

Who is your competition?

Your competition for good talent is not your main adversary down the street. It is every industry *outside of insurance*. These people have more options than ever before. In most cases, they are young, inspired, anxious to work, and very smart. This may not sound like the generation you have heard about (see upcoming section on Generations in the Workplace), but the reality is that these people are really no different than you or I were at their age. They are ready to get on with their careers. And, they might be at a point where they are still in search of that career. Your job is to make insurance (and you) an option. And that won't be easy.

Working in insurance

What is it that might attract a young and bright person to gravitate towards a career in insurance? Unless they had a parent or other relative in the insurance business, it's unusual for them to have dreamt of selling universal life insurance as a youngster. The glamour and simplicity that technology has brought makes it much more attractive to work in other industries. Your task is to turn insurance from portly to sexy. Here are a few ideas…

- **Attend high school and college job fairs.** Get a table or booth and hand out information about the benefits and contributions of insurance. This is NOT a place to pimp insurance…it's a place to recruit! Educate young people on what insurance is (risk transfer to protect peace of mind and lifestyle). And what it isn't (professional football players showing up for career days). Promulgate the rewards so that you become a viable option.
- **Hire interns.** This is a low investment for you, but offers a tremendous amount for both parties. You get some work done that is better suited to be performed by a low- to no-wage earner (hence, intern), or work for which you don't have others with the necessary skills (social media guru). For them, they get valuable work experience that looks good on resumes and applications. They might also find they like the industry!
- **Offer to speak at schools.** Schools are always looking for business partnerships. Offer to give a presentation to a business class at the local high school or community college. You can speak about insurance as a career, or insurance as a highly necessary and important cog in society. Either way, you are advancing the notion that insurance isn't all about guys in white polyester pants and slicked back hair trying to pull a fast one on the unsuspecting victim. You have real business value to give at a pro bono level. You will see the reward.
- **Volunteer at school events.** Even just being visible has advantages. You get the opportunity to interact with kids and most often you have a chance to talk about yourself, your career, and the rewards.

- **Get your young agents out in the community talking.** A peer talking to peers is always the best. If you have young agents in your office, have them go out to schools and talk about insurance jobs and why they should be considered. I never talked to anyone about insurance as a career until Barb was hired as a receptionist for an agency. I may have listened to a recent graduate talking about her experience and why she was happy.

Now you might be saying, "Dan, there are loads of new people entering the industry every day. Look at the numbers of insurance agents out there already!" This statement has merit to it. As of 2010, there were almost 500,000 insurance professionals in North America. Unfortunately, the average annual revenue was a paltry $47,000. That means that agents either were not trained well, or were in the wrong business. Not everyone is cut out for it. That being said, if the industry itself can do a better job on the front end, the back end may just perk up a little! You know that old adage, "garbage in, garbage out." The principle works in reverse. If you feed the right information out about your industry, then the results will be brighter applicants.

Working for you

Now they are interested in insurance. The next step is to have them interested in you. I hold executive breakfasts for insurance agency principals frequently and this issue of recruiting talent is often a topic of discussion. I will ask my guests to name off reasons for working for their agency. Here are a few of the standard responses...

- Great health benefits
- Strong 401K and investment options
- A sound and competitive salary
- A chance for advancement
- Training programs.

While all these bullet points are good "benefits," they are not "reasons." There is nothing wrong with this list. In fact, many of you will hire people based on these benefits. The real question is how long can you keep them? It's expensive to hire someone new. It normally takes 18 months before you, as a business owner, break even on your investment. Many people leave jobs within that first 18 months because they don't like the business, the work environment, you, or even worse, are bored.

I encourage those attending my breakfasts to change their language. You should have a value proposition for why people will stay and flourish by working for you, just you have a value proposition as an agency that sets you apart, . How you do this is by peeling away at the onion. Let's take those five bullet points above and try to answer the question you should ask of any company "benefit:" *So what; who cares; what's in it for me?*

- We offer a diversity of options to keep you healthy. These include a strong medical insurance program that we pay for, not you. In addition, we include a free membership to the local health club for all employees as we value your health and well being. (Great health benefits.)
- We offer you the opportunity to accelerate your long-term financial future so you won't ever have to be concerned about money. The choices are many, but the decisions on your future are yours. (Strong 401K and investment options.)
- We pay our people really well because we pride ourselves on hiring only the best. We never equivocate on salary, as we know we return our investment on the quality of our people. (A sound and competitive salary.)
- We have no glass ceilings at this agency. You hold your career in your own hands and we encourage, endorse, and promote your growth both professionally and personally. (A chance for advancement.)
- We don't let our employees struggle or fail. We ensure that we provide all the tools you will need to accelerate your career and advance as quickly as you want. (Training programs.)

Some of you might be thinking, "Dan, you're just adding some big words and spin doctoring what the original benefit was."

> *Definition*: Spin doctoring is the fine art and manifestation of being a "spin doctor." A spin doctor is defined as "a person who provides a favorable slant to an item of news, potentially unpopular policy, etc, especially on behalf of a political personality or party." (Courtesy of Dictionary.com)

I'm not. I'm adding the real value to those benefit statements. The key is to be able to verbalize them (verbal is both oral and written communications) with sincerity and genuineness to potential employees. This is not an act (i.e. spin doctoring), but this is the real belief that you are improving the life and condition of another by converting them into an employee of your agency. If you don't believe that, you will be quickly "found out," usually at your own cost and peril.

The bottom line for you is that simply hiring people for the sake of hiring is a painful way to go about the process. You want to hire people that stay, that add to your internal culture, that help your business flourish, that help your clients and customers, and people that you're happy about when they walk in the door to work. You know the difference. Approach recruiting and hiring with that mindset.

The big takeaway

If you only take one thing away from this chapter, it should be this (have your highlighter, pencil, or finger poised to notate…)

Hire people, not positions.

Not very complicated, but really hard to do. Think about your own hiring practices. If your receptionist quits, you need to hire a receptionist. If one of your CSRs wins the lottery and never comes back, you need to hire that position. I understand that needs and specific situations like this occur, but in the end, it's not an ideal way to build a team and create a culture for your agency.

Maximizing talent: How mentoring programs cultivate success

Mentoring has existed in the insurance industry probably dating back to those Chinese and Babylonian businessmen. Somebody had to pass on the knowledge and smarts about finding the right risk transfer method to ensure their boats crossed safely, right? The problem for insurance agencies has been that the mentoring program has been less defined that it is in the company carrier world. Patience, time, and resources are in short supply yet the need has never been greater.

The process of creating a formal mentoring program may seem steep. It may also seem unreasonable if you're part of an agency where everyone is maxed out to the gills with work and duties. That being said, it can and needs to be done. While this topic could be a book all by itself, I do want to touch on a few simple strategies. It's these strategies that will help you develop a painless and easy to implement process to at least get you started down the right track.

1. **Take the time to write it out.** Informal mentoring programs don't work because they don't last without real accountability. Whatever you decide to put into place, write it down. You can always amend, adjust, and adjudicate later.
2. **Ask for people that do want to mentor and then compensate them.** Some people have no desire at any level and would make crummy mentors. You will find at least a few that have a spirit of helping others succeed. These are your mentor candidates. They need to be compensated in some way. Financial is a default, but not the only method. You can consider things like extra days' vacation, gift cards to restaurants and getaways, company recognition, and/or airline miles. Be creative. I promise you the small compensation investment you make will be returned many times over by better employees and results.
3. **Train them.** Most people have only mentored their kids and that's not always the best example of skilled business mentoring! There are plenty of ways to train them – hire a professional trainer (I taught mentoring skills to the United States Navy); get video trainings online; buy books by experts in mentoring; use webinars and teleconferences and online courses. Somehow you again need to invest in making sure your mentors are set up for success. I reiterate that the return will be worth it.
4. **Set up a support group.** I'm not suggesting therapy. I'm suggesting a regular confab to share ideas, continue trainings, contribute successes and challenges, and even just vent. Their regularity can be monthly, but they are really necessary for the continual growth of your mentors and their continued desire to remain mentors.
5. **Set expectations.** Create a template that informs everyone from mentor to mentoree what the *rules of the road* are. This involves frequency of meetings and calls, topics of discussion, length of mentoring, ability to get out if it's not going well, structure to continue working together if there is synergy, and the formality of the relationship. This can be as detailed as you want. I recommend it does not delve into minutiae, but is complete enough to deal with common situations This should be a living document that gets kept up to date and revised as needed.
6. **Get feedback.** Feedback should be taken from both the mentor and the mentoree on a consistent basis (e.g. quarterly). Action should be taken on reasonable requests and ideas.

7. **Don't give up.** It's not always easy at the beginning, and other "priorities" may pop up that take you away from monitoring this program. If you've ever been part of an initiative that got started with much fanfare and eventually dissipated to die in apathy or other "priorities," you know it's really hard to ever get it back. This is where agency leadership has to be resolute in its commitment to the betterment of the agency.

Bottom line – If you have an agency of over five people, you can make this work. If you are under five people, the agency owner or office manager will need to take on the responsibility. Regardless of your agency size, the importance of mentoring is important to the continued success of your agency.

Generations in the workplace

> *"Now the good old days weren't always so good, and tomorrow's not as bad as it seems."* Billy Joel from his song *"Keeping the Faith"*

Allow me to begin this section by stating that I am not an "expert" on generations in the workplace. I have many colleagues that are and have written books on the subject. At the end of this section, I will give you their names to follow up if you like. That being said, somehow or another I find myself stuck in between generations and consider myself an authority on at least the two ends. This section is to not provide you with all the answers to working together among four generations (it might be five depending on who you listen two –and that is a problem in and of itself).

I was born on December 31, 1964. That auspicious day marks what generations experts proclaim is the last day of the "baby boomer" era (1946-1964). My wife was born exactly 3 months later on April Fools Day in 1965. (Note that she was born on a day that everyone plays practical jokes on and I was born on a day when everyone celebrates with alcohol, kissing, and fireworks. Just saying…). Whenever we are in a disagreement, I feel I can accurately proclaim that she doesn't understand me as we come from different generations. She doesn't find this amusing, but I do.

In actuality, I am more suited to the morally corrupt and selfish Generation X (1965 to 1979) it seems, rather than the American Boomers born of the Depression and World War II era who later became hippies at Woodstock and birthed the technological age we live in. Ironically, my parents had me late in life and my father lived through the Depression as a child and served in the Atlantic in WWII.

My dad and I had a terrific relationship…after I turned 21 or so. As a kid growing up in the 1970s and early 1980s, he had plenty of trouble with my long hair, bell-bottom jeans, and Van Halen albums. His reality and experiences just didn't line up together. Even as our relationship grew closer as I matured, we still saw the world through different lenses.

This phenomenon is not uncommon in the workplace. Books upon books have been written about generations in the workplace. People have been branded, folded, filed, and mutilated in the name of understanding how we can all work better together. It seems that the thought is that just because of when we were born, we will have a more difficult time adjusting and understanding each other.

I respect my colleagues who delve into this world, as I do believe there is some credibility to generational similarities and differences and ways to leverage that. For the sake of this book and for you, I want to make this as painless and useful as possible.

Hence, I give to you the ***Dan Weedin 10 Rules of Generational Relevancies***.

1. **People should never be placed into generational boxes.** While I admit that generations do have tendencies, so do dogs. The people you employ should be judged on their behavior and activities, not on the year in which they were born.

2. **Don't overthink this concept.** The reason people behave as they do more likely correlates to where they lived, what they did, their parents, their experiences, and their prior work. While you might consider generational generalities, don't weigh them too heavily.

3. **Don't assume because it was good for you, that it's good for your younger employees.** Just because you had to walk to work in three feet of snow without any shoes and were thrown to the insurance wolves to fend for yourself, doesn't mean that that's what will be best for them. Seriously, your way of learning or "work ethic" may be badly outdated.

4. **Speaking of work ethic, stop complaining about the new generation's lack of gumption.** This stereotype has existed since Julius Caesar complained his kid didn't have the killer instinct he had at his age. I find it very ironic that the "Boomers" of this era are calling out the new kids on the block. They at one time were hippies with flowing locks, living free, and jamming to Jimi Hendrix, Janis Joplin, and Bob Dylan. Those "rolling stones" are now throwing stones. While there are plenty of young people who lack motivation, that is true of every generation. It's not a generational problem; it's an individual malady.

5. **Be willing to learn from them.** They know more than you in many areas – specifically technology, social media, prevailing communication platforms and what motivates young insurance buyers (their money is green, too). The best thing that you can do is to leverage the power of their minds and in so doing you will engage them and build loyalty.

6. **Train them.** This means mentoring, accountability partnerships, and formal training with experienced people in your office. The results may surprise you. Your mentors may actually improve more than your protégés. In the meantime, those young guns will learn the business and possibly find some perspective in dealing with us old veterans!

7. **Ditch any remnants of command and control.** In the "old days," you may have had to grin and bear it because you had few options. Not so today. These young people are able and willing to leave if they don't find their work or environment rewarding. They know you're the boss. Earn their respect through collaboration rather than asperity.

8. **Age is relative.** I have been giving center stage to the "young" talent. That is now changing. We should probably change "young" to "new." I did a project with the Department of Defense recently. The project was to teach supervisors and managers how to become strong mentors. As art of the class, we had some "new" leadership development people interspersed so they could learn, too. While the majority of these "newbies" were young, one that caught my attention wasn't. In fact, he was a couple years older than me. Turns out he was building up a new career after retiring after 30 years in the Navy. He was back in school so to speak and considered one of the new influxes of talent. Gone are the days when someone in their fifties or sixties can't contribute. You may well find that some of the very best new talent has a little gray sprinkled in their hair. You may find that the manager is younger than the trainee.

9. **Get help if you need it.** Sometimes there is a chasm that needs to be crossed. The root cause may be generational, but I tend to think that might be only a part of the problem. My colleagues are able to help organizations deal with issues related to diversity in generations. If you think this is the issue, don't try to fix it yourself. Just like you'd never operate on yourself, you need to get help from those who know most here.

10. **Educate yourself.** Out of those throngs of books, there are some good ones. You might learn a thing or two. If you're going to be an effective boss or manager, it helps to be armed with knowledge and a multiplicity of opinions.

Bottom line – diversity in generations in the workplace, your workplace, is here to stay. People will be working longer because they are living longer. There is value in what they can teach. There is also value in what they can learn. Make sure you have provided the environment and the culture to thrive.

Resources:

Roberta Matuson

Matuson Consulting

www.MatusonConsulting.com

Anna Liotta

Resultance Incorporated

www.resultance.com

Chapter 9
The Errors of Commission

Changing the game in producer compensation

Creating a conflict of interest

I'm an avid golfer. I've been traipsing around the links for over 35 years and my rounds have been either walking the course, or using a golf cart. In all those years, I'd never used a caddy (although I had been one), until August of 2011.

I was in Bogota, Colombia, at a major executive conference where I was one of the keynote speakers. My mother is a full-blooded Colombian and I had not visited her native land in 40 years. This was an ideal opportunity to mix business with the pleasure of reacquainting myself with my family after four decades. One of my cousins is married to a newspaper executive and a fellow insatiable golfer. He invited me to join him and our other cousin on the links at his club. How could I say no?

To my surprise and delight, Bogota does not boast golf carts; they have caddies. Part of it may have been that we were at a posh club but, according to Jorge, this was not unique. You never saw carts. Jorge hooked me up with an extraordinary young dude, named Sebastian, as my caddy. Sebastian was awesome! I am certain his guidance and attention to every detail saved me six strokes that day. Heck, he even found two balls in play that I had given up for lost. If I had the capacity to stuff him in my suitcase and bring him home, I would have done it. I am certain my handicap would have plummeted into single digits!

How do golf caddies get paid? They may have a base stipend, but tips are the dominant part of their compensation. (I was lucky that my money was no good with Jorge; he took care of Sebastian for me.) However the size of the tip is usually commensurate with the experience, not the score. Let's face it, we all like posting a low score on the golf course, but if we end up having a terrific time and enjoy a remarkable experience, the caddy gets paid well.

Can you imagine if the caddie was paid in inverse proportion to your score? In other words, the higher score I shoot (bad for me), the more the caddy gets paid (good for him). As the golfer in question, every "read" and suggestion couldn't be trusted. It would be to his advantage to increase my score to raise his reward. Crazy, huh?

Yet isn't that exactly what we do in compensating our producers?

As an agent, I hated bringing bad news to clients on renewal. Ninety-nine percent of the time, the bad news at renewals revolved around increased premium.

During the late 1990s, contractors started seeing huge premium increases as a consequence of construction defect claims. I had a sizeable book of both residential and small commercial contractors. They had been living the "good life" when it came to insurance for years. Every preferred carrier had a special program for contractors, both general and artisan. And man, were they inexpensive! As agents, we had "the pen" in many cases. We could very quickly and simply quote a contractor on a ***BOP-type policy***, close the deal, and bind coverage in the same day without the underwriter ever seeing it.

> A ***BOP-type policy*** is insurance gibberish for Business Owners Policy. This is a bundled package policy for select classes of small business, and includes Commercial Property, General Liability, Auto, Crime, Business Income, and other bells and whistles not normally included with a conventional policy. BOPs tend to be broader in coverages and scope, less expensive, yet also not available for all small businesses.

Contractors, who are notorious for price shopping because they are used to the bid system, loved life. Construction was up, and insurance prices were down. Then came that game-changing peril called "construction defect."

Insurance carriers were now beginning to be named in lawsuits which they had never thought they would ever be involved in. Due to defect claims, attorneys were naming everybody from the painter, the landscaper, and the carpet installer for mold-related claims. Carriers started panicking. Some carriers wanted out and immediately stopped insuring contractors. Others that wanted to wait it out, drastically increased premiums and reduced coverages. Over the course of several years, more carriers withdrew as premiums rose and competition dwindled. The old supply and demand curve had collided with pure panic!

Construction was still good at first, so my contractor clients didn't just go out of business. In fact, business boomed. They had higher revenue and labor costs. Those two factors are the critical rating basis for General Liability. It was the perfect storm for both the contractors and insurance companies – increased premiums based on higher revenue or labor, plus less opportunity in the market.

I still remember walking into one client's office at renewal to deliver the bad news. His premiums were going up by about 30% and there were no other options (The good news for me was that every agent was in this predicament). This was a guy who trusted me and we had built a strong relationship. I empathetically said, "David, I'm sorry but your premium is up 30% and we have no other options. I'm really sorry." And I was. I also cringed at his response.

"Dan. I knew this was coming. It's not good news for me. But, I guess you just got a big raise, huh?" He had a wry smile. And, he was right. My income was based on a percentage of his premium. When it went up, so did my paycheck. I had to admit that this in fact, was the case. I so intensely wanted to remind him that during years of a "soft market," when competition is high and premiums drop like a lead balloon, I would lose significant money just in order to save an account. I thought better of it. I didn't blame him. I was not only *not sharing in his pain, I was directly profiting from it.*

The insurance transaction

There are three parties in the insurance transaction. All have the same desire (no claims or losses), but different objectives.

The ***insurance company's*** goal is about achieving bottom line growth. The company wants to bring in more premium dollars than they need to pay for claims and operations. They are required to meet certain levels of being above that line to be considered solvent and able to do business.

The ***insurance agent/broker*** wants to sell accounts that produce high-priced premiums because his or her commissions are a percentage of those premiums. The more premium dollars sold and the higher the commission income from the company carrier, the more money they make. Plus, the more premium he/she sells, the more potential contingency income he/she receives from his/her companies.

The ***insurance buyer*** wants to get the best coverage at the lowest price.

In basic terms, the insurance agent, who is trying to build trust and rapport with the insurance buyer, has an objective that is counter to his client's. This is never a good recipe for a trusting, collaborative partnership. In fact, it is a key factor on why there is so much perceived animosity in the business.

Commissions make little long-term sense for insurance professionals because you deal with annual renewals. If you're a car salesman, you sell the car and you're done. While you'd like to hope you get return business, it may not occur for years, the person is likely to move out of the area, and you may not even be in the business. While you may be at odds during the negotiation, your business partnership is probably limited to about 20 minutes. Not so in insurance. Your objective is to keep this client for many years. Their renewal pays the agency the same amount every year, so it's critical to long-term sustainability. Why would you set up any appearance of an adversarial situation?

I understand that commissions are the way things always have been done when compensating insurance agents. Agency owners feel it promotes motivation for acquiring new business and for hunting "elephants"– the jumbo accounts. They feel that this is the superior way to inspire activity in agents. While some of that may be true, it undermines the relationship with all clients. As competition has intensified due to technology, and an increasing number of companies are finding ways to squeeze out their agents, forging sustaining relationships built on trust and mutual objectives is a necessity for agent success in the future.

Good for the producer

Why is it good for the producer, you ask? Doesn't commission-based compensation reward your big hitters, your "rock stars?" Yes…and it can also demoralize and drive away young talent that may not have had a chance to maximize their skills.

If you're an agent, think back to when you started. I will always remember my first day in August of 1989. No computers (at least not by today's standards), no cellular phones, no Internet, no Angry Birds. I was given a small desk with a rate book that I had to use manually, a chair, and a pen. "Go get 'em, son!"

And I did fine, as did all of you. My point is that I had almost no training and was sent out to eat what I killed. Today, that's not a very good formula for success for a young producer. Even if you start them on a salary basis, the end result is moving them to commission only. As new producers (they aren't always young any more) work into that level of compensation, the chance for hard times increases.

Anxiety and desperation minimized

Anxiety and desperation are two known killers of producers. Fear masks talent. In my early days as an agent, there were many times I thought my family would starve if I didn't sell an account. Of course, that wouldn't happen, but just the presence of that anxiety was detrimental to my ability to sell at that moment. Anxiety, fear, and desperation cause bad things to happen:

- Pressing too hard for the sale – prospects can smell it like a lion on the hunt
- Taking short cuts or even cheating that leads to Errors & Omissions issues
- Paralysis (mentally not physically, although you never know)
- Loss of confidence

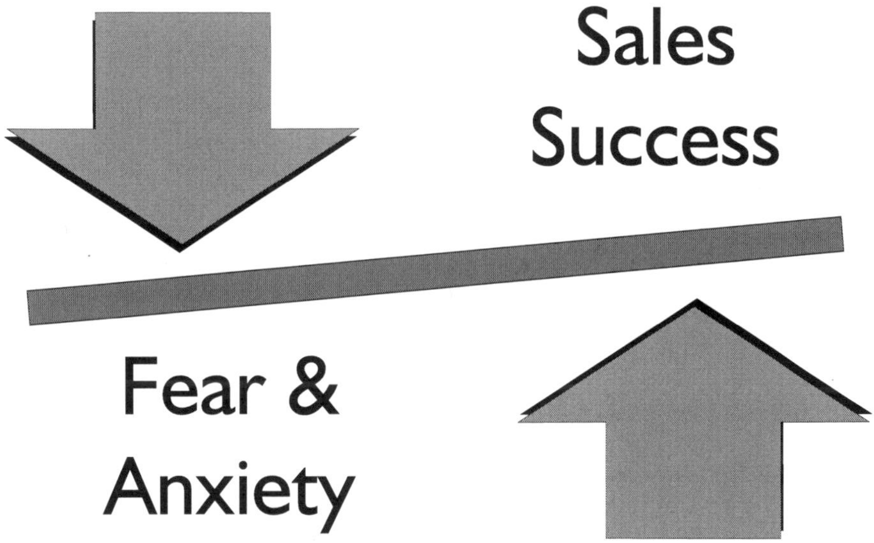

Visual 9:1: When fear and anxiety increase in a producer, the consequences are decreased sales success

It's a slippery slope when that happens. Sales managers and agency owners often become inpatient and allow good, young talent to walk out the door. Ultimately, poor training, non-existent mentoring, and a compensation program that only rewards based on premiums could be the downfall of a good career and expensive to the agency.

Loss of elephants not demoralizing

Many "rainmaking" producers got that moniker because they picked up very large accounts – jumbo accounts known as "elephants." They are awfully fun to get because in a commission-based compensation system, it's big money right up front. Even renewals are healthy chunks of one's income.

The problem is that losing one is devastating.

I watch *Mad Men* on television. In the fourth season, the advertising firm's largest client (by far) left the fold, causing a ripple effect of devastation in its wake. Consider one producer losing a major account like that; it might take years to get that revenue back.

Certainly, losing a jumbo account on a salary-compensation schedule is no fun at all. However, the anxiety and disaster of the situation is mitigated in knowing that his or her salary is not going to be ravaged. With the economic calamity of 2008 and beyond, many large companies have merged, been sold, or just gone out of business. In my consulting practice, four out of my five largest clients were sold or ceased to exist within a three-year period. When a producer's book of business goes through the swings of an economic disaster and reduced premiums, you can go from "rainmaker" to being rained on very quickly. That ends up leading back to anxiety, fear, and desperation.

On a brighter note

I mentioned a couple of issues related to the negative – fear, anxiety, desperation, and loss. Let's be more positive.

- Producers who are more confident are more likely to win more accounts. Confidence is king when it comes to sales situations.
- Producers will be more open to collaboration and sharing.
- Young talent will be more motivated to grow and stay.
- Ability to increase salary though incentives still remains.
- Relationships with clients are enhanced leading to a higher renewal percentage.

Greg Collins is President of Parker, Smith & Feek Insurance near Seattle. Mr. Collins' agency has never used commission-based sales in its 75-year history. During an interview I held with him, he mentioned that their renewal percentage historically runs at

95-96%. This is 5 to 6 points higher than what is acknowledged as excellent in the industry. He credits much of that to salary plus incentive based compensation.

He believes the system is set up to strengthen relationships because producers aren't solely focused on new business acquisition where commission splits are higher; more attention is paid to the existing clients.

According to Mr. Collins, *"People are not coming to a business to earn a paycheck. They want a sense of purpose and fulfillment that manifests itself into how supportive they are of clients. Compensation systems and cultures encourage them to do the right thing for clients."*

Good for you

As an agency owner or principal, you have a lot to worry about. Employees and issues dealing with them usually come to the surface first. The legendary business guru, Peter Drucker once quipped, "Culture eats strategy for breakfast."

Producer compensation is not just about the producers. It radically affects the entire organization. According to Mr. Collins, his agency has a much higher level of collaboration and teamwork due to the system. Nobody is worried about solely themselves and their personal bottom line. As I will discuss later, they are incentivized to work together for the good of the team. How can that not be good for the agency? The investment made in that will be returned many times over with increased efficiency, higher morale, and increased income.

Good for your client

I guarantee you; most of your clients don't have a clear idea of how you get paid. They understand there is a level of commission and that you share in it as a producer. That point by itself should concern you. As with my example, they understand that when their premiums increase, so does your bank account. This can never lead to a true partnership. They must hold the genuine belief that you have their best interest at heart always. Even when the hard market hits and their rates go up. Even when you're proposing additional coverages (that are in their best interest) that substantially increase their premium.

This will be an point of issue with clients. Think about when you go into buy a suit or a fancy cocktail dress. If you had the choice of working with someone on commission or someone who was on salary, which would you choose? Both might take you to the same expensive rack. However, you might think differently about their motivation to do so. Is it in their best interest or yours? Your clients are bound to feel the same way. During my seven years of working directly with business owners on a consultative basis, they have indicated this. It should make you worried about long-term relationships.

> *Note*: Just in case you're wondering, as a consultant I work on a value-based fee concept, not hourly. Because of the same conflict, I would never allow my clients to think I was taking longer for my own agenda, or that I was calling them to add time to the meter. Relationship is everything in business, and you need to avoid any perception of trying to feed yourself first!

How to seamlessly implement in your agency

Salary-plus incentive-based compensation and an insurance agency seem like a painful combination. Depending on your current set up with producer agreements and staff, it might be. However, if you're willing to make a paradigm and culture shift in your agency, it's worth the battle.

The following template is a "game plan" for making the switch from commission only to value-based fees. My guess is that every step of the process can be challenged with, "It can't work because (fill in the blank)!" That might be true. Change is never easy. It will be met with resistance. That's where leadership comes in.

Step 1: Producers need to buy in

If you have rock star producers, this will be your first major hurdle. You need to convince them that it's in their best interest to make a change. Here are a few talking points...

- Offer to make the transition over a 12-18 month period. You can negotiate terms on what might be incentivized beyond normal production. You can consider keeping a certain percentage of the top business on commission for a certain period of time. Be creative and talk with them.

- Offer to start them with a base salary of what they made the previous year plus a 5% or 10% bump. This gives them some peace of mind in a volatile market.
- Get creative with incentives. At Parker, Smith, and Feek in Seattle, Mr. Collins offers different incentives to different producers. Here are a few examples – community involvement, mentoring, industry involvement and awards, thought leadership, public speaking and publishing.
- Offer to pay them for their lowest 15% in their book of business. This will free up time to find new business, yet they get a bonus of money plus the salary that included those renewals.

> *Note:* There are many small- to medium-sized agencies where the main producers are the agency owners or are salary incentivized. These will be an easier transition.

Step 2: Make a plan and be prepared to explain

This must always be about WIIFM (What's in it for me) for your employees. If they understand this change is in their best interest, then they are more likely to play nice. You need to take time to plan this out, discuss how everyone (even non-producers) will be incentivized, and how the organization as a whole will be improved. Generating excitement is your ultimate goal.

Step 3: Avoid Gravitational Pull

What is gravitational pull?

It's the basic human instinct to go back to the default position when things get dicey or busy. For example, you might decide that you're going to change your eating habits to lose weight and be healthier. You're motivated and ready. For 30 days you stick to your plan and you start seeing some improvement. Life is good!

Then, you go on vacation and visit restaurants. It's hard to stay as committed because everyone else is eating things you can't. Vacation is followed up by a holiday period. Food with all sorts of smells, visions, sugar, and carbohydrates is swirling around your senses. Your default position is to eat it all. You tell yourself you will go back to the plan next week, but it's too late. Gravitational pull has returned you to your original state, and far away from your desired state.

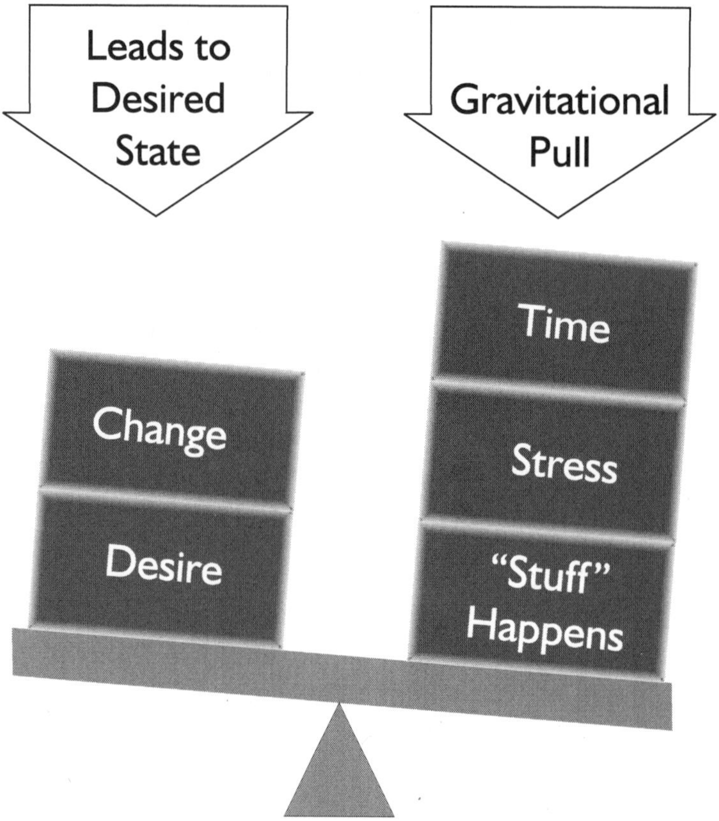

Visual 9:2 - Gravitational Pull is when the challenges of the day keep pulling you away from the changes you want to make over time. They slowly drag you and your quest for improvement down.

Whenever you implement something new, there's a honeymoon period when everyone has "bought in." At some point, business as usual puts pressure on the new culture and, unless it's stopped, will drag everyone back down. Producers will complain, CSRs will complain, you get tired of playing bad guy, and you ultimately capitulate. You've wasted time, money, and a good thing.

You stop gravitational pull by first realizing that it exists. Understand the factors and triggers that start it. By being able to visualize what those triggers are, you can set up a plan to put little bounce factors in place to "bounce" the team back up.

One note to always remember. You have to be committed and passionate about the change. This is an essential requirement in change management. The first sale is to yourself. Be sure this is what you want to do, and don't allow anyone or anything to drag it down. There will be challenges. That's why you need to remain strong.

Challenges

I'm not naïve enough think that there are no challenges with this system. It's not foolproof. I asked Mr. Collins what his perspective was on challenges and here's his list...

- Continual pressure and tension with transparency. You know producers share notes on what people make and what incentives they might have. You need to be prepared as a leader to nip those things in the bud; mitigate any damage; be a strong communicator; and ultimately stand firm while still being fair.
- Control of compensation.
- Disagreements with judgments and performance in subjective areas.

There may be more, and probably are. Mr. Collins' agency has never known anything different and that makes it easier to deal with. Implementing a major change like moving from commission compensation to salary plus incentives will add more speed bumps.

Step 4: Keep changing

You never get anything completely right the first time. This will be no exception. You will see some of the challenges I just detailed. Be prepared to be creative. Ask your team for candid feedback and suggestions. Don't be defensive, yet stand firm that this is the new way. Too often, it can be a *"my way or the highway"* situation. The old *command and control* tactic is no good in building consensus and culture.

Being a change agent has its headaches and speed bumps. However, you have often been a change agent with other initiatives. You just haven't thought about it that way. Be prepared for the push back and have answers, or at least be prepared to ask for help.

Contrary to what you might think, the larger the agency, the easier this will be. You have many smart people in your organization. The answer is always in the room. From a larger group, you will get more ideas and more push back. Both are good. You will also find that you have a proportionally larger group of non-producers who might actually be on your side promoting this. In smaller agencies, you may have a 1:1 ratio of producers and support staff. If you are a good influencer and can persuade the masses that this is in their best interest individually and collectively (which it is), then you may have a whole squad of evangelists!

Step 5: Monitor

Even as you change, don't take your foot off the gas pedal. It's imperative that you monitor the success, and don't let your guard down, even if it seems everything is good. You remember that famous line from former President Ronald Reagan about the Soviet Union and the nuclear arms race? He declared that we should, "Trust, but verify." You should, too. Keep tabs on your producers...Are they happy? Are they reaping the rewards you expected? Are your producers' sales numbers increasing? Is your renewal percentage climbing?

One of my clients is a genius when it comes to collecting data and then leveraging the power of it to enhance operations and success. You should be keeping data, too. Find out where the weak spots are. It would not be uncommon for your team not to notice, as it's not all empirical evidence. The data you keep – and it doesn't have to be complex or time consuming – should tell you whether your objectives are being met. You determine what your filters are and then keep track. Time will tell if you are being as successful as you had hoped.

Brand spanking new

If you are a new agency, or you ever start one, this is a great template to begin with – using sales plus incentives compensation package. You may be small when you get started and it might be easy. It might only be you as a producer, but as you add employees and producers, you can shift right into this model without having to go through any paradigm shifts with your team.

Bottom line

In the end, your success and reputation as an insurance agency will be based on the job you do for your clients. In today's world, clients have the ability to find more options when it comes to insurance than ever before. Personal lines business is already there with self-quoting web sites, 24-hour service, and lizards answering your calls. While it may never get there with commercial lines, you still must acknowledge that the industry has changed and continues to evolve. Consolidation and mergers of agencies and companies will continue. What makes you unique?

Relationship is everything in business. You must always be working in step with your clients as a team. The major problem for the majority of agents is that they are viewed not as a partner, but as a necessary evil. The fact that the amount you get paid has nothing to do with the value you provide will eventually do more than irritate your clients. You may see them ask for a change. Heck, the fee scandal from a few years ago that former New York Attorney General Elliott Spitzer propagated turned a much closer gaze at fees and the industry. There is no turning back.

Salary-based compensation is a win-win-win proposition. The producer has greater confidence in what they earn, yet can still be motivated with higher incentives. You as a principal owner or executive get to maximize the talents of your team, improve collaboration, and ultimately enhance your reputation. And your client knows that you are working in their best interest always, which leads to longer sustained relationships and business.

> *Note* – before you tell me they don't all think that way, remember that you lose some business every year. If everyone loved you, that wouldn't happen. The fact that Greg Collins and his agency get a substantially larger renewal percentage means that they can focus on working more efficiently and better meeting their clients' expectations. Think about it. It's harder to acquire new business than to keep it on the books. Build the relationship and make more money.

Insurance agencies, due to merger and acquisition, are becoming more and more the same shops with different names on the signs. How do you differentiate your value and service? How do you rise above the white noise? You create a culture of value-driven, relationship-based sales backed up by a collaborative, efficient team.

That's the formula for long-term success and happier clients and employees.

Chapter 10

Who's on Deck?

Perpetuation and succession planning strategy for agency principals

Prelude: So you're not an agency principal...yet. Or maybe you never want to be. This chapter is still important for you to read. Why? First, if you eventually want to have ownership, you need to be active in the adjudication of how ownership is parsed out. You can have a huge impact on ownership by letting them know you're interested. You might be a key player in forming a program. The time to act is now, before any other decisions are made and they didn't know about your interest. If you never want to be an owner and you are a key team member, your own self-concern for future employment would predicate the need to know what the agency plan for perpetuation is. If you like working there and want to continue to even if the current ownership exits, you need to be part of the conversation. Knowing what the process looks like is in your own self-serving (not bad in this case) interest.

One of the great joys of my life was coaching my daughters in youth sports. It also taught me more about life than I think I even realized then, but that's for a different book.

One particular year, I got to coach the mighty 8- and 9-year old softball all-star team. My daughters Mindy and Kelli were both on the squad. Somehow, I finagled Barb to help coach on the bench. I figured a terrific mom was an ideal bench coach! Little did I know the power of 8-year-old girls.

I was in the 3rd base coaching box keenly concentrating on the runners on base and the player at the plate. This, as you might imagine takes acute concentration. As I'm deep in softball strategy, I hear Barb call my name. It started with a whisper and was beginning to rise in tone and timbre. Of course, I had greater things to deal with, but I decided that I should see what all the commotion in the dugout was about. I turned around and saw Barb holding Kelli by the shoulders while the rest of the players on the bench were gathered around her trying to pull something off her hand. Kelli had somehow lodged her pinkie into the teeny, tiny little hole on the top of the batting helmet. Even the efforts of one mother and 11 teammates weren't getting that digit dislodged! It resembled the action that you might see on a Saturday morning Looney Tunes cartoon with Bugs Bunny and Daffy Duck!

To make matters worse, Kelli was on deck. For you baseball neophytes, "on deck" means that she was the next batter to come to the plate after the current batter either reached base safely or was retired. When it suddenly became her turn, my 4'5" daughter with a batting helmet affixed to her pinkie was not in any position to go to bat. The umpire approached me and bellowed, "Batter up!" I had to explain to him the situation. While it was clear he found this amusing, the rule states that she had to bat next. All of a sudden, as if the most powerful lubricant of all time suddenly drenched her pinkie, the helmet became dislodged. The result was one very red and swollen pinkie. Her attempt in the batter's boxed fared no better. Unmotivated and hurting, she limply gripped the bat with one pinkie extended as if she was at high tea with the Queen. She made three listless swings and struck out. Kelli trudged back to the bench, quite satisfied that her appearance at the plate was over, and determined never to stick her pinkie in a helmet again.

Kelli was the "on deck" batter. Her job was to be in a position of readiness to step into the batter's box and get a hit. Like most 8-year-olds, she got distracted and the results were not good for her or the team.

Who is your "on deck" hitter to purchase your team (agency)? Are they ready to step into the batter's box and deliver, or are they distracted? Waiting too long to determine your own exit strategy will leave you limply swinging at fastballs with your pinkie protruding.

In my experience, small- to medium-sized agencies have done a less than exemplary job of preparing for the egress of their owners from their business. In the old days, fathers would wait for their sons or daughters to buy their agency, get paid a handsome amount over time, and live the good life of retirement. This formula worked for a long time. Today, the influx of children even wanting to be in insurance has diminished. The competition, technology, and cost have driven many to seek other careers. That leaves only a few options, and you know how 'supply and demand' works.

Regardless of the type of agency you own or work for (captive or independent), perpetuation is critical to the entire team. If the principal sells to anyone outside of the family (including internal team members), everyone's future is called into question. These are the few options most principals face today:

1. **Sell to a true family member like a son, daughter, nephew, niece, etc.** That still happens today, but the son or daughter is probably demanding some sort of security that their investment has a fighting chance for continued success.

2. **Sell to an internal team member.** Whether you think it's right or not, this option usually means the rock star producer. They are the ones that an afford it and have provided the revenue generation for the agency. The bad news is that rock star producers often don't make even "garage band" leaders or managers. Without good training, they may put the entire agency in jeopardy.

3. **Sell/Merge with a competitor.** If both parties are relatively strong, align in culture and dynamics, and have the same vision, this can work in either a merger or sale. I've been part of that process in the last agency I worked for. The down side is that even with all due diligence in place, change can be hard and there is always a concern about trying to force a solution for viability.

4. **Sell to a Big Dog.** National brokers are always searching for a good book of business to buy. They consider this a key organizational strategy for growth and why not? It's the quickest and most profitable way for them to acquire new business. They may even offer principals decent terms for buyouts and allow them to ride off into the sunset for a few years. This is becoming more of the norm, as the first three options usually have greater risk.

5. **Sell it back to the company.** For many direct writers like Allstate, Farmers, and State Farm, this might be the only option. The company will buy it for whatever the contract decrees, and then eventually find someone new to buy it from them.

Interesting note. The agency I began working for in 1995 was a small shop with five employees. We merged in 2001 with a similar sized competitor in the same city. Culture, vision, and the stars all aligned and it made sense. The agency ran smoothly for over a decade until they "merged" with a national broker recently. The principals are all still what I would consider young and now work as employees. The decision was most likely the best one for them and their employees to remain competitive for the long run. It's getting harder to compete unless you have dynamic market presence, powerful branding, or a specialized product. Even those with the best intentions sometimes find that they have to make midcourse adjustments. The moral of the story is that this highlights the gravity of proper succession planning.

When and how?

The question of when to start your exit strategy is an interesting one. For the younger agency owners (my definition is under 55 years old), it seems fanciful to even consider an exit strategy. Why, you have lots of years left to race this horse, right? For those who are more "mature," by the time they think about it, they may have waited so long that their ability to maximize their return on investment is diminished.

Advice from Earl Bell

Earl Bell is a Seattle-based expert on increasing business value, personal income, and maximizing your ability to "spend" your discretionary time the way you want to. Earl has worked as a Chief Financial Officer for numerous companies throughout North America for nearly 20 years. His prowess is in reducing the time it takes for business owners to improve profitability and increase the company value to prepare themselves for exiting.

I asked Earl to describe what warning signs might be catalysts for younger agency owners to start thinking of their own exit strategy. He said,

"As baby boomers continue to age out as a group in the coming years, the number of agencies up for sale will dramatically rise. According to an article in Inc. Magazine published in April 2008, An estimated 65% to 75% of all small businesses will go up for sale in the next five to 10 years. Why? Retiring baby boomers." Now if you follow simple math and go back five years to when this article was written, a glaring conclusion is that the tidal wave of business transference has already begun. Predicting the timing of waves in the ocean is not an exact science, but you know the waves are coming. The same can be said for the impending supply of insurance agencies that will be up for sale; this is going to happen soon. Basic rules of economics dictate that when supply increases in excess of demand, then prices decrease. To use the beach and ocean as a metaphor, two key questions to ask yourself are…. *"Do I want to get caught up in the big wave that is coming AND when is it time to get out of the water and off the beach?"* My advice is to carefully assess the strength of your agency today and determine its value. The next step is to determine: (1) what needs to happen in order to maximize the ability of your agency to predictably produce the same level of income without your active involvement (in other words, the agency is sellable at maximum value) and (2) how long this realistically will take. Finally, the art behind this science is to assess the timing of your personal risk/reward ratio and determine WHEN it makes the most sense to sell your agency, assuming this is part of your personal financial planning strategy.

Earl's advice is sound and his analogy of the waves is fair. If you're a young owner, taking the time to strategize now, before it's too late, is the whole basis of risk and crisis management. Following the same readiness and preparedness logic that you impart to your clients on an insurance basis should be a part of your own planning. A little introspection and perspective is always a good thing!

I also asked Earl to provide some advice for those more "seasoned" agency owners who might find themselves on the downside of the wave with a wobbly surfboard. What kind of approach can they implement at this stage of the ride. Earl's response was,

An alternative strategy for maximizing value in your agency is not to sell the business immediately but instead sell to employees over a period of time. During this ownership transition period, the required involvement for you as an owner will eventually evolve from *absolutely necessary* to *non-existent*, which ensures a smooth transition for clients, you and the new owners.

Agency transitions are inherently risky. As a mature owner, you have built long-term relationships and clients who want to do business with "you." If you are near or past normal retirement age, it would not be uncommon for employees to think they can simply leave and start up their own agency. While some clients may follow, many are loyal to you and would seek your advice on who can best serve them. Chances are you wouldn't give a glowing referral to employees that leave and betray you. So alternatively, why not design a solution that works best for everyone? To illustrate, you could sell ownership in the agency over *a few years* to key employees, based on certain criteria such as time or achieving certain operational milestones. Buyers eventually take over running the agency by assuming your professional responsibilities and client relationships. Clients have 100% transparency that the transition is designed to take everyone's best interests into consideration – most importantly theirs! Selling your agency to employees is a good approach to take when a strength of relationship and high level of trust exist between the owner, employees and agency clients.

While Earl is an expert in exit strategies and I agree with his comments, this can be easier said than done in this industry. Normally, it takes a special situation for an employee to be able to afford or want to buy your agency. It most often occurs with high-earning and successful producers. If you're a smaller agency, you might not have one of those! The next most common employee is the family member, which we touched on earlier in this chapter.

Since family members getting into the family business has been a common practice over the decades in insurance, I queried Earl for his thoughts on selling the agency to a son or daughter. I asked him specifically to discuss the pros and cons of this type of transaction. Here is what he said:

Buying and selling an agency is an emotional process for all parties. Emotions can easily become amplified when familial relationships become intertwined with agency needs. To help provide a broad overview of what typically can happen, below is a list of indicators to help identify when selling to family members was either successful or not successful:

Signs that selling to next generation family members was *successful*:

1. As an owner, buyers are well suited to assume agency responsibility and each buyer has clarity regarding their employee role/responsibility in the agency and how decisions are made without the seller's active involvement.
2. As a steward, buyers are capable of running the agency so that sufficient income can be passed along to the first generation owner and support their retirement.

3. As an agency operator, buyers can either maintain, enhance or evolve agency culture such that strong relationships with clients, vendors and fellow employees are maintained or improved upon.
4. As a family, buyer and seller can get together for family gatherings without stress and drama at the dinner table because the ownership transition went smoothly.

Signs that selling to next generation family members was *not successful*:

1. As an owner, buyers are not well suited to assume agency responsibility because of inability to navigate the transition from family to agency relationship, owner vs. employee role, or boss vs. underling responsibility. Remember, in an agency, someone has to become the primary decision maker! With new ownership, this person is no longer the patriarch or matriarch of the family.
2. As a steward, buyers are not good agency operators and as a result, the seller needs to come back to run the agency. This undoubtedly will increase and not decrease stress levels both at the office and at home.
3. As an agency operator, buyers destroy agency culture and cause harm to relationships with clients, vendors and fellow employees. When clients, vendors and employees all talk in unison about longing for *the days of the past*, there are significant challenges to overcome for both business and family.
4. As a family, buyer and seller cannot sit at the same table for holiday dinners.

When selling to family members, and strictly from a financial perspective, a good accountant, wealth advisor and attorney can help structure the transfer of ownership in a way that is tax-advantaged and best positioned to ensure the best financial answer for your personal situation. However, and in my opinion, it would be foolish to focus strictly on the flexibility of terms and income tax effect that selling to family members can provide compared against selling to non-family members. A much larger problem than income tax planning can arise when buyer/seller fail to proactively manage all potential pitfalls resulting from a sale to family members.

The important thing to recognize is that the inter-personal dynamics involved with family ownership at the next generation level require heightened skill building around the areas of creating effective collaboration among siblings and in-laws. When it comes to generational transfer of agency ownership, the initial instinct is often to focus on assessing the technical capabilities of each family member and then delegating responsibility in areas such as new business development, marketing, operational matters, accounting or office administration. However, the more important skills which increase probability of success are more adaptive and relationship driven in nature covering areas such as building communication systems based on trust, teamwork, accountability and the alignment of goals and vision. I would be remiss in not mentioning that nearly 70% of business transfers to a second generation of family ownership fail. The failure to proactively seek help navigating the many pitfalls associated with mixing family and business is a primary reason for this unfavorable statistic. Having said that, 30% of families have successfully transferred ownership of business interests to the second generation. While in the minority, these families invest time, energy, focus and passion on preserving, sustaining and building strong family connections, governance of family and business interest, leadership and management over business operations. My advice to you is to study and learn from the 30% who have been successful, or seek advice from professional advisors that help families navigate generational transfer of business interests."

Your terms

The problem with succession and perpetuation planning is that it feels an awful lot like selling Life and Long-Term Care insurance. It makes us come face to face with our own mortality. Even if you are still young, it requires that you advance your life at breakneck speed to the end. That's a hard thing to do for any of us.

You always need to know the "end game." The "end game' is a chess strategy that moves the game into the final stages for a victory for one person. The "end game" of any basketball play drawn up by the coach always results in a made basket. In both chess and basketball, the "end game" is strategic. It always boils down to execution. In your case, we like to term this implementation.

In order to win your "end game," you'd have to know what it was if you tripped over it. What does it look like and how does it feel? Here are 10 questions you need to consider and answer honestly to yourself regardless of what stage of ownership you're at:

1. **At what age do I want to exit this business?**

   You should at least pick a number. It doesn't have to be carved into granite – more like sand. You can change based on the economy, the situation, and your level of fun. But at least have a destination in mind so you can plan out one of the questions coming up!

2. **Do I want to sell and ride off slowly into the sunset or leave immediately?**

   Some agency principals sell (or transition) and leave immediately. Some, on the other hand, are hired by the new owners to manage their book, write a little business, and act as a consultant or coach. What would be ideal for you?

3. **What do I want to do *after* I exit?**

   This is the second part of the age question. You should know what you want to do. I do and I've got several decades left. Do you want to travel, write the Great American novel, learn new languages, drive a race car, or simply relax at home in your garden? Or, perhaps speaking and consulting are new challenges you feel you'd like to tackle to keep you young and vibrant. Again, you can have plans that are fluid…but you need to start somewhere.

4. **Do I care to whom this business goes to as long as my clients are taken care of?**

   If the answer is NO, this doesn't make you a bad person. Your clients and employees are your concern, but as long as they are adequately tended to, that might be enough for you. On the other hand, selling to a competitor or national broker makes your skin crawl. Whom do you want to see your legacy attached to?

5. **Is there anyone currently on my team that would make a likely successor?**

   The usual suspect in this question tends to be the rock star producer. They are generally the ones with the financial ability and tenacity to take the reins. That being said, never overlook managers and other key direct reports (especially in a larger firm) that you would identify as strong leaders, In the end, the money may buy the agency, but it doesn't guarantee leadership or management skills.

6. **Are my children or other family members interested in the family business?**

   It seems that in the "old days" this was more common. To a large degree, it still is. As I write this book in the summer of 2013, I have three current coaching clients that have either purchased the agency from their father, or have plans to do so within a three-year time period. Often, kids go off to college and university to become the next great nuclear physicist, novelist, or technology guru. Then they emerge four years later thinking that this insurance gig isn't so bad, especially because they can get a job right away! Even if your kids balk at the suggestion in their formative years, use your intuitive powers to guess if they might later actually be a candidate.

7. **What are my retirement financial goals and how does the value of the agency play into that?**

   Your ultimate ability to gain true wealth (discretionary time) lies within your bank account. Money isn't true wealth, yet is the vehicle that funds it. Your agency's book value, lines of business, and repute will all play a factor in the selling price. You should begin extrapolating out into the future and estimate what agency value you need to reach to assure your vehicle to true wealth. And, don't forget to factor in cost of living, inflation, and volatility.

8 **What do I want any transition to look like in regards to my future employees?**

   Your employees of the future (depending on your exit date) are important. They have families and lives that are dependent on you. Any transition or change impacts them greatly. From a purely humane standpoint, you need to 'ensure and assure'. Ensure kindness and professionalism in how they are treated, and assure some plan for income continuation. Making your employees a key element in your strategy is the right thing to do for them and for the ultimate value of your agency.

9. **What do I need to *stop doing now* that is hurting the value of my book and the attractiveness of my agency?**

   Many experts talk about starting and so will we (see #10 below). I also advocate for scrutinizing what you should stop. Here are three recommendations:

- Stop making bad hires. Easier said than done? Check out your own hiring practices and confirm there are no flaws.
- Stop taking on bad clients. Just because they have the ability to write you a check doesn't mean they are a good client. No bad client is worth the money because they end up draining you of it. Ultimately they will damage your loss ratio and your agency's value.
- Stop procrastinating on strategizing. If you're a ways out from your grand exit, start by taking one hour a month solely for the purposes of creating an exit strategy, doing research, and working with professionals. That's a minimum of 12 hours a year. That will end up potentially being the most valuable investment you can make for your future discretionary time!

10. What do I need to *start doing* that will enhance my book and the attractiveness of my agency?

This is implementation and it's the least sexy part of this process. Here are some of my "start" suggestions:

- Start setting metrics on your eventual exit. Be specific in goals, objectives, values, and time frame. Write them down and view them regularly. Be free to make adjustments as necessary.
- Start recruiting for potential buyers. This might seem ludicrous if you're decades away, but you never know when opportunity presents itself. Even if not in the near term, people you meet now may be the one that is interested (or could refer) later on. In addition, the person you recruit for your agency may be the heir apparent. When you hire and meet new people through continuous recruitment activities, it's amazing how "lucky" you get!
- Start building a team that is attractive to buyers. Don't take offense to this. You might have terrific people already in place. I can confirm that I have never been in an organization where I was an employee, that didn't have some weaknesses in human capital. That weakness could be either a poor or underperforming team player, OR the lack of a skilled person to fill a vacant or needed role.

What's stopping you and how to move forward

In over a quarter of a century of being in this business, the topic of perpetuation always comes up. The gravity of this issue has always seemed to be in the forefront of the minds of agency principals. The problem is only a small percentage of owners get off the dime and make progress. This section is going to be short and sweet, yet hopefully a catalyst to get you moving.

The speed bumps

- Lack of urgency.
- Apathy.
- Complacency.
- Poor priority setting.
- Fear.
- Ignorance. (Don't know where to start.)
- Arrogance. ("Someone will certainly want to buy my agency so I don't need to do anything now.")

The road grader

- Sense of obligation to your family, employees, and clients.
- Scheduling skill.
- Covenant to keeping commitment.
- Outside help. (Consultant, coach, expert.)
- Paradigm shift that this is part of your job as principal.

The bottom line is that you need to commit to the activities listed above and convert vision into action. I'm not so naïve as to think it's easy. But owning and managing an agency isn't easy either. This is part of your job, and you must take it as seriously as bringing on new clients, companies, and staff.

BONUS: An Interview with Don Bielen, Director of Business Advisory Services for The Rainier Group in Portland, OR.

Don specializes in ownership transitions, business succession and wealth management for successful business owners and affluent individuals. Since 1992, Don has successfully completed well in excess of 100 business transition and succession plans for clients throughout the United States. He works closely with Rainier Group clients and technical staff to provide direction and consultation to design and implement advanced planning strategies. He is recognized by his clients and other advisors as a trusted, knowledgeable, organized and creative leader in his field and community.

Donald received a Masters degree in Business Administration (MBA) from the University of Oregon and holds a CFP® designation as a Certified Financial Planner™ practitioner. He received a Bachelor of Science (B.S.) degree in Business Finance and a minor in Economics from the University of Montana. He is also a graduate from the College for Financial Planning in Denver, Colorado.

Dan: *Why do you think business owners wait too long before thinking about and implementing succession planning?*

Don: Their identity is tied to the business oftentimes and they equate succession planning to their retirement from the business and fear losing their key relationships and their sense of self worth. Secondly, they are consumed with day-to-day operations and/or challenges in the business and don't prioritize succession planning, therefore, they continually delay succession planning because there is no perceived return on their "investment" and feel their time is better used elsewhere. The most common mistake is that they equate business succession planning to a transfer of their ownership, involvement and control of the business and don't want to lose control of their largest financial asset and potentially their financial security. Finally, business owners delay because they are unsure as to whether the next generation is skilled and capable of "taking the reins".

Dan: *If you had an exit date in mind to transition out of an agency, how many years in advance would you need to plan? In other words, help me understand the "working backwards" model.*

Don: I would need three to five years to address the following:

1) Determine what I need from the business to meet my financial needs relative to the value of my ownership.

2) Determine how best to realize my value without jeopardizing the company's financial viability and

3) Prepare the next generation of leaders and owners to run and manage the business and leave it in capable hands.

Dan: *If someone realizes they need to start now, what's the best first step?*

Don: Define their personal objectives in terms of financial needs, involvement in the business (retirement goal) and objective for the disposition of the business (keep for family or employees, third party sale, or liquidate).

Dan: *What are the most overlooked factors in succession and perpetuation planning?*

Don: Matching the skills, passions and dreams of the next generation with the skills and required capabilities of running the business. Said differently – passing the business to the next generation for the wrong reasons.

Dan: *What advice would you give agency owners that think their children might want to succeed them?*

Don: Help the children better understand what is required to run, manage and finance the business so they have a clear idea of what they are buying off on and make sure the children understand what it took to start and grow the business – the key lessons learned over the years of growing the business.

Dan: *What's the biggest mistake business owners make in the planning and strategy process?*

Don: Lack of objectivity in the planning process by letting emotions, family expectations and personal pride obstruct their ability to plan ahead and effectively evaluate the next generation and their fit with the business.

Chapter 11
Jumping Out of the Plane

How and why to become an insurance consultant

It was 2004, and something inside of me said, " I need a change." I wasn't sure what it was and I hate when that happens. I enjoyed insurance. However something about the grind of being an agent for over 16 years was getting to me. It wasn't going out and marketing, or meeting with clients and prospects. It wasn't the business. I knew I enjoyed helping people protect the livelihoods they had worked so hard to carve out. I needed a catalyst to help me understand what it was and what my next steps were.

I was working as a successful commercial agent for a good agency. The people were terrific, I was treated well, and I had a lot of autonomy. What I didn't have after 10 years was ownership, and there seemed little chance that this was going to happen. I have an entrepreneurial spirit, and I like to make my own decisions. I also like to keep the majority of the money I earn for my life, not my bosses. One of the first things that became apparent was that I needed to be my own boss.

What I didn't have was a desire to own my own agency. I had a three-year non-piracy agreement on a book of business I had worked 10 years with my current employer to cultivate. I would need to hire employees, which I wanted no part of. I knew there were tons of rules and regulations, which I would have to keep up with as an agency owner. Small is difficult in gaining insurance company carriers to give you an agency appointment. And, I really didn't want to delve into the captive agency scene (State Farm, Farmers, Allstate, etc.) because at that time, these companies were primarily personal lines, life, and were soon to move into other financial services. That wasn't my deal, as I had spent 95% of my efforts over my 16 plus years as an agent in commercial lines property and casualty.

The catalyst for me came during several interactions with long standing clients. These were really strong clients, who knew and loved me (and I felt the same). My agency was of medium size and had a decent range of companies it represented but, it couldn't always compete with the big boys. All of a sudden, I found myself getting competition from agencies that had created specialty programs, and they were marketing aggressively to many of my better clients. On these occasions, my clients would come to me and say, "Hey, Dan. We received this quote from another agent who says they have a special program. We trust you. Would you look it over and tell us if it's legitimate? *It probably isn't any better than we have, and we know you will give us the straight scoop."*

Unfortunately for me, it not only was legitimate, but it was better than anything I could offer. The premium was always significantly better (not just barely), and more importantly, the coverages improved my client's condition. I had to honestly tell them the truth. They were always grateful. And, then they fired me.

It was never personal. (In fact, after I became a consultant, they became my first clients!). They asked my opinion with the trust that I genuinely had their best interests at heart. In return, they received information that forced them to make a good business decision. What I hated was that after building a strong relationship with these clients, that relationship actually led to them leaving me. Could I figure out a way to do both? I began to think after this pattern replayed itself several times, "I wonder if I can make money doing this?" And so was born the idea of becoming a consultant.

I began to research the idea and was humbled to see that it wasn't the first time somebody had thought of this concept. I found a guy who was on the opposite side of the country from me who had started a consulting practice six years earlier after a long career as an agency owner. Scott Simmonds out of Saco, Maine, soon became my mentor and accelerated my start in the consulting world. Many of the tips, techniques, and strategies that helped me get started, I will share with you in this chapter, along with a few words from Scott in my interview with him.

A final note to my story, which I believe is important – I make quick decisions. (While sometimes my quick decisions come back as swings and misses, more often than not, I get base hits!) I did my research and contacted Scott in May 2005. My decision to become a consultant had already been salted away and my resolution to go with Scott as my mentor to help me lead my new career was easy. What I couldn't do was lead a double life as a guy trying to sell insurance for my agency, and in the background working on my practice. Your head needs to be in one place, and so I knew I had to tell my bosses.

They were really good about it, and actually knew that I might be of value to them in my new role. We worked out a deal for me to help them transition my book to new agents, carry health insurance on me, and allow me to start the process of working on my practice. This deal was for 60 days. By the time the 60 days ended,

I had my first client at a $20,000 fee, and they had smoothly transitioned my book to reduce the chance of losing any of them as clients. To this day, we have strong relationship and have been able to collaborate and refer business to each other. It was a triple win. That is how you want to transition from one job to your new career.

What is an insurance consultant anyway?

Not everyone understands exactly what an insurance consultant does. This is especially true of your consulting prospects! While all consultants can create whatever practice they want, let me provide my observations based on my practice, and those whom I have learned from. This is not meant to be exhaustive, yet it does provide the key differences that I believe separate the two.

- ✔ Consultants don't sell insurance. They are an unbiased insurance professional that is not influenced by commissions or agency contracts.
- ✔ Consultants work on a fee basis. I highly recommend value-based fees over hourly billing. If you choose to go the consulting route, I can explain this practice in greater detail. For this book's purpose, we work for fees paid directly to us by the client, rather than commissions paid by the insurance company.
- ✔ Consultants focus on improving conditions, changing behaviors, reducing administrative burdens, developing strategy, and implementing of projects.
- ✔ Consultants can be flexible. In other words, we can do just about anything that is asked of our clients, even if it involves work outside of the insurance realm. Agents are tasked with placing coverage and focusing on activities around this. The ability to offer a myriad of services doesn't often work from a revenue and profit standpoint.
- ✔ Consultants tend to be more project-based. While I have had clients who have had a continuing, unaltered relationship with me, easily over 90% of my clients work with me on individual projects. They have a need; they hire me; I solve the issue; and then I move on. I've had many clients that I've done several individual policies for. Agents who are used to ongoing relationships where they have little work to do after the sale must get used to doing shorter, more intense and focused projects.

Is consulting for you?

There is a reason that there are more insurance agents than insurance consultants. Perhaps the biggest reason is client need. What I mean by this is that business owners must buy insurance. They may be required to in many cases. However business owners at least have a cursory idea of the value of insurance for protecting their assets. They may not like paying for it, but they understand they need it. Agents have a captive audience. They don't have the same need to hire a consultant. Consultants (at least the ones like me who do not sell insurance) are initially looked on as an additional "cost." The biggest objection faced is, "Why should I hire you if I have an agent?" We will tackle that objection later in the chapter.

Being a consultant has both its challenges and opportunities. It also demands a certain mindset and skills that not everyone has. This is true for anyone wanting to be a consultant, not just insurance. Let's determine right now if this chapter is going to be useful to you by telling you what kind of personality and skill set is needed to be successful in pursuing a career as a consultant. If after reading this section you decide that consulting isn't for you, feel free to pass GO, collect your $200, and advance to the next chapter. This is a unique chapter meant for those of you who want to look at options in your career, either now or in the future. If it doesn't resonate for you, feel free to move on.

Anatomy of a consultant

Business insurance focus

The truth is that to be successful as an insurance consultant, you're going to need to focus on business owners. This can be Property & Casualty, Workers Compensation, or Health & Benefits. Dealing with individuals is simply not going to give you the ability to charge fees that will make your practice profitable. Individuals just don't have the same need. While you might create some intellectual property that helps individuals (I have many articles and videos), these really end up being ways to spread your brand as an expert. Your market is the business community and you must be adept and comfortable with this clientele to start a consultancy.

Ability to work solo

My office is three paces from my bedroom. I have no employees, no water cooler, and no distractions. It's just the dogs and me, and they rarely make any noise unless they hear a squirrel or the garbage truck outside. The silence can be palpable. You have to be able to deal with no other interactions outside of your daily conversations with clients, prospects, and other business contacts. You must be focused. I mean really focused.

Recently, more and more agents are being moved out of the office and into their homes. This transition may be much easier for agents today than it was for me. I was fortunate in the sense that my children were in high school and I didn't have to deal with child care. I have many colleagues that have that added distraction of dealing with smaller children. This requires even greater focus. It's not a deal breaker, but it will test your ability to successfully work from your home.

You're in the marketing business

The sales cycle in consulting is hugely different than in insurance sales. There is much less sense of urgency for your prospect. As an agent, your sales cycle is greatly determined by renewal dates. There is urgency when that date comes up, and there is a definite lead-time needed to get a quote and provide it in ample time for a prospect to make a decision.

As a consultant, you will find times where your prospect has a huge sense of urgency, and that is because something bad happened and they need you to clean up the mess. More often, you must build your value, your credibility, and ***create a need***.

Consulting is ultimately about marketing, not selling. I have always advocated that cold calling is inefficient and wasteful to your time as an agent. As a consultant, those two adjectives are exacerbated. You have to tame your aggressiveness for a sale, eliminate "pitching" from your vocabulary, and focus on alternate ways to quickly improve branding to gain "at bats."

Other chapters in this book define and discuss marketing versus selling. I won't belabor that point here, other than to say if you can't convert from selling to marketing, you will have a harder time converting prospects into clients.

You must be a continuous learner

I was an agent for over 16 years and I can say the following with full clarity. Outside of wanting certain designations and being required to keep up on continuing education credits, I didn't aggressively seek out educational opportunities to improve my craft. You can't do that as a consultant. Since the beginning, I've had mentors, coaches, attended intensive classes, and joined Mastermind Groups. And that doesn't involve anything dealing with insurance! All of my professional development dollars (outside of licensing requirements) have been invested in improving my ability to be a strong marketer and acquire business. Period. This is a tough business and you need to be better at marketing and developing your brand than even your area of expertise. My assumption is that if you're reading this, you're probably pretty good at what you do and you are an expert on insurance. That's not really what being a consultant is all about. You have to prove to others that you can help them significantly improve their condition, and that means learning how to effectively find and influence prospects.

You must have high self-confidence: The first sale is to yourself.

In 2009, I attended my first live event with my professional mentor, Alan Weiss. Though I had worked with him over the phone, this was the first time I'd met him or seen him in person. I will never forget one of the things he told the group. The class was titled 0-300, and was how to get your business from zero revenue to $300,000 in revenue quickly.

Someone asked him what the most important difference between us taking the class and those consultants earning really high revenues was. He quickly responded by saying, "Self confidence. All of you in this room (about 35) are very good at your areas of expertise. You might even be better than the million dollar consultants. But, they have significantly higher self-confidence that transcends everything and allows them to gain more clients, take more risks, and accelerate growth."

You may think you have high self-confidence. I did, too. But I learned that my confidence was not as strong as it needed to be. It became essential to increase my confidence and to be willing to be more edgy, be willing to make people angry, be willing to be disliked, be willing to lose business, to know in my mind that I have tremendous value, and to share that with people, and finally to truly believe that I was the expert. I had to eschew the cliché that the customer is always right. I am the expert…I am the one who has the right solution. This was an evolution that took time, introspection, and courage.

There is a difference between arrogance and self-confidence and it's important. Arrogance is the internal perception that you are the best at what you do, and you don't need to learn any more. You know it all. Self-confidence is the feeling that you are the best at what you do, and that you still have more to learn to thrive at being so. People with high self-confidence never stop learning and continually look for ways to be better for their clients and themselves.

Burning the boats

When Hernan Cortes traveled across the Atlantic Ocean to the New World, he had one thing in mind...building a new life in this New World. Legend has it that upon arrival in the new country, Cortes ordered the boats burned as to not tempt the crew to quit and go back home. With that "easy out" removed, it was all about survival.

You have to have that same commitment. You have to be willing to "burn the boats." It's very easy to get discouraged, especially in the early going and when challenges outside your control adversely affect you. You must have the mindset to persevere.

Now, I'm not going to suggest that you go bankrupt or become destitute. If you don't like consulting, if it's not in your DNA; or if things just don't work out, there is no shame in building new boats and sailing to other lands. You have to do what you have to do. What I am telling you in this section is that you can't go into this endeavor thinking that you have an "out" if it doesn't work out. You must believe that it will at all costs. This is too tough a business, and it's too easy to quit. Go in believing.

The sales cycle paradigm shift

One of the biggest paradigm shifts I had to make going from a successful sales person to a consultant was how I viewed and attacked marketing and the sales cycle.

Here are the main differences you must understand between an agent and a consultant.

1. **Your buyers aren't required to buy what you're selling.** We discussed this earlier in the chapter. Unlike insurance, which is considered a "necessary evil," the burden is on you to create a need that they don't know they have. This is not an easy task. Because of this, the sales cycle is longer because it takes longer to create need, build trust, and be influential. By the way, the bigger the client, the longer the sales cycle, unless you already have a strong relationship or a strong referral.

2. **You can't rush the sale.** With insurance, you normally have the backstop of the expiration date. Agents are also trained that you need to try and close the deal before you walk out the door. There is (or at least was to me), a full-court press mentality. In consulting, it's a half-court game (to keep with the basketball metaphor). You can't rush into a proposal just because the prospect allows you to. You must, and I emphasize MUST, have a conceptual agreement with the prospect on what their objectives, metrics, and values are before you draw it up. Otherwise, your chances of successfully sealing a deal are vastly reduced. In insurance, this isn't a requirement or deal breaker. Rushing through the process was my biggest challenge and, in all candor, was the issue that took me the longest to overcome.

3. **Your buyers may be different.** As an agent, my economic buyer was always the business owner – the President or CEO. As a consultant, the CEO is rarely your buyer. More likely, it's the CFO or COO. As a consultant, it's even more valuable to be able to quickly determine who your buyer is. They are harder to recognize. (Note, if you're working with small business – under $20M in revenue – you are most likely dealing with the President and founder of the business.)

4. **Emphasis on value over methodology.** In insurance sales, agents tend to be very focused on a few areas, notably premium. While I acknowledge that successful agents do a good job of maximizing their value with risk management, unique expertise, and special customer service; the emphasis of most sales by insurance agents is focused on premium and the methodology that agencies provide. Methodology is defined as service work that the insured can expect in return for their premium.

   In consulting, the almost total emphasis is on value. Value is defined as return on investment, results, and the improvement of the client's condition. The language used by the consultant always moves away from fee and towards results. Consulting buyers try very hard to find out price. But what they really need is how they are improved. If they are going to receive an extraordinary ROI, then they will buy. I guess you can say the difference boils down to agents deal with *reduced premiums, while consultants deal with increased value and ROI.*

5. **Diagnostic vs. Prescriptive.** Agents often must be both diagnostic and prescriptive. Insurance sales is more than just coming up with the lowest premium. It also involves analysis of perils, risk tolerance considerations, and the uncovering of gaps. Consider this example…

   Agent Smith is working hard to influence Ms. Jones, his buyer who is President of a $75M manufacturing company. During the prospecting period and before the official proposal, Agent Smith discovers that there are gaps in coverage dealing with Business Income for Dependent Properties. Mr. Smith finds that they need coverage for a key vendor, but they have none. In an effort to impress, Mr. Smith tells Ms. Jones about the gap and she is grateful. No matter what happens over the next period of time, Agent Smith always has the leverage that they found the gap. It should be used boldly in sealing the deal.

   This type of thing happens often. Agents must give out prescriptive information because as in the case above, time was of the essence because a very important gap needed to be closed. Sometimes, in the case that urgency is not an issue, it might be saved for a more important time in the sale. Regardless, being prescriptive and diagnostic is required.

   In consulting, consultants often give away too much methodology or advice for free. It's fine to give some basic information, especially in the form of diagnosis. Getting too prescriptive can lead to buyers taking the information themselves and going at it alone, sharing information with competitors, or lessening the ability to charge a commensurate fee. This part of the sales cycle is different and must be learned by the consultant early in the process.

What kind of services can you offer?

Remember earlier in this chapter I told you that there needs to be an answer to the question, "Why do I need an insurance consultant?" This is where you get that answer!

While the concept is to provide value, there is methodology involved that isn't (or in many cases can't) be done by agents. This section will give you both. You will first see the methodology, and that will be followed by the value.

Insurance audits

Methodology

I call my third party audits "Insurance Fitness Exams." The methodology is providing a comprehensive review of a client's insurance policies (regardless of the type – commercial, personal, life, etc.). You have no dog in the hunt, so your focus is on your client's wellbeing. The report you provide will discuss the good, the bad, and the next steps to gain improvement.

Value

Clients have now significantly improved their ability to save money, enhance protection, and assure business continuation. They also have an improved peace of mind, which in the end may be their biggest value received!

Broker selection

Methodology

Many insureds do regular "shopping" of their insurance. While they may end up doing it for all the wrong reasons, you can help them. This happens by managing the process – reaching out to agents to offer proposals, scheduling and facilitating interviews, delivering specifications, handling all questions from agents, offering suggestions and recommendations, and follow through on policy issuance.

Value

A reduction of the administrative and executive burden for your clients. Somebody has to do all this work. If you take this off their plate and provide a professional perspective, you might be their hero.

Risk assessment

Methodology

Performing on-site risk assessments of risks and hazards. This includes walkthroughs, interviews, and perils analysis.

Value

This is all about making your client more attractive to insurance carriers to ultimately reduce their premiums and enhance their protection.

Outsourced risk manager

Methodology

I've done this for several clients. They are too small to have their own internal department, yet they are large and complex enough to need the help. You act as the liaison between the agency/company and your client.

Value

Reduction of administrative burden again. While this normally isn't a full-time job for them, it's enough of a distraction for them to keep them away from doing other important things, plus it takes them longer and they may not do it as well. You provide them time back and a better product.

Crisis management

Methodology

Perils analysis, facilitation of strategic work, review of current program, and implementation of solutions. Insurance (risk transfer) is only one part of the crisis management program. Prevention, control, and response are also included.

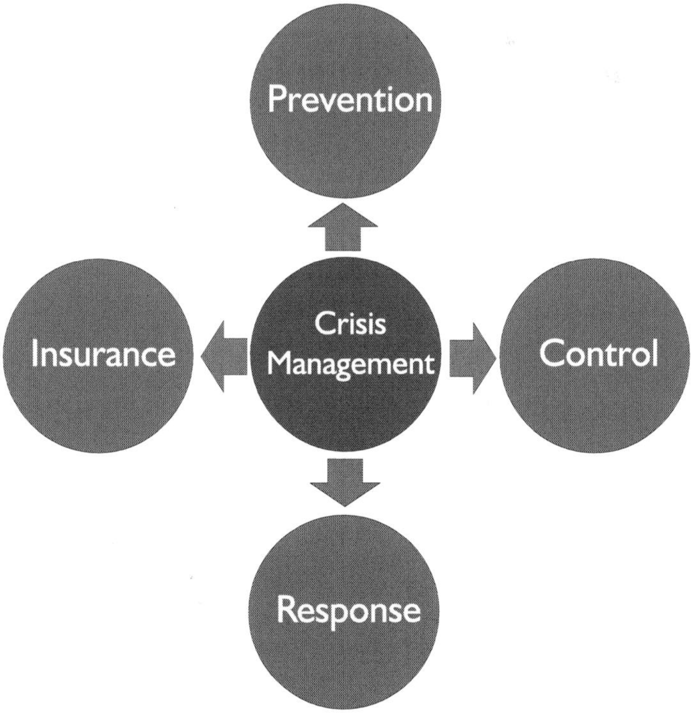

Value

They are dramatically more likely to prevent the huge known and hidden costs of a crisis. They experience improved employee morale, more content investors, happier clients and customers, and relieved supply chain partners. Most insureds do a horrid job of crisis management. They basically rely on a combination of insurance and "seat of your pants" to make it through. By offering this service, their biggest value is that something just never happens. This can be a tough sell, but those who have endured a serious crisis, understand it.

Coaching and mentoring

Methodology

Providing access to your smarts. Business owners, executives, and risk managers need your smarts whether they know it or not. At the very least, these folks rarely have the insurance background. In most cases, they don't understand the risk process and you can educate them. This can be done on a retainer basis or one-time fee.

Value

You've helped them improve their decision-making process. They can make important decisions that include risk much more quickly, more astutely, and with more peace of mind (there's that phrase again). Smart business owners like making decisions, but the most sophisticated ones like to use a team of experts. Most don't have that internal expert, so your filling that bill is immensely valuable.

My Interview with Scott Simmonds

Scott was my very first mentor and had a profound impact on where I am today as a consultant. He left agency life as the principal of an agency in 1999 and has built a highly successful practice near Portland, Maine, as an insurance consultant. You can learn more about Scott and his work at www.ScottSimmonds.com.

Dan: *What was the driving factor for you to leave a successful career as an agent and start your consulting practice?*

Scott: An agency purchase deal had fallen through and the agency was bought by a bank. I stuck around for a year – with the president of the bank telling me that someday I could be president of the bank. I woke up one morning and thought, "Why on earth would I want to be president of a bank?" At the same time I wanted to build my own business. I came up with the idea of an insurance expert who did not sell insurance.

Dan: *What was the toughest challenge for you in the first six months? What did you have to do to overcome that?*

Scott: I knew I wouldn't make the same money I was making selling insurance for a few years. I built a plan and budgeted for basically no money coming in for a year.

I did a great deal of wheel spinning trying to attract clients – cold calling, attending networking events, buying advertisements. I finally settled on using my accountant for referrals. The first few years my accountant's fingerprints were on more than half my projects.

Marketing is the number one focus even now. I have consistently spent 20% of my time in marketing.

Dan: *What are the three most important distinctions in the sales process for consultants and agents?*

Scott: I don't sell insurance – I'm unbiased – I don't accept commissions from agents or insurers.

We will talk about things your insurance agent has never talked to you about and I'm going to make your insurance easier for you.

Dan: *What is the biggest mistake newly minted consultants make coming out of agency life?*

Scott: Waiting for the phone to ring. You can build it – they will not come. He who has a thing to sell, and goes and whispers in a well, is not so apt to get the dollars, as he who climbs a hill and hollers.

Dan: *How do you know you shouldn't consider consulting as a career, and stay as an insurance agent?*

Scott: Look at your sales activities over the past two years. If you are selling because someone handed you the business or marketing because someone had told you to. Stay put. Internal motivation trumps everything else.

Dan: *What are you doing in your practice today that you weren't doing when you started 13 years ago?*

Scott: Focusing on a single industry – financial institutions. I can say with certainty that I know more about bank insurance than a prospect's insurance agent. Three hundred financial institutions and counting.

Dan: *What is the most significant personal reward you've attained as a consultant?*

Scott: Freedom and I keep what I kill.

Quick Start Guide

Okay, so you're intrigued and made it all the way through the chapter. You have more than a 35,000-feet interest in consulting and you want to make a move. Here is your Quick Start Guide to making the decision and then moving forward.

1. **Consider your options and make a decision.** This isn't rocket science or mining plutonium from Mars. This is about the following questions you must honestly answer:
   - Where are you financially (can you survive without any revenue over the next 6 months)?
   - What kind of support do you have at home (will your spouse or significant other be willing to support you through the peaks and valleys of the early part of your practice)?
   - Do you feel like you can work by yourself? This isn't so easy for everyone, or his or her spouse/partner. You need to be focused and resist the urge to wash and fold the clothes when you should be writing an article or preparing for a speech.
   - Do you possess the skill set to be a consultant? This may be hard to answer now, but hopefully this chapter has helped you determine that.
   - Do you have the passion (most important)?

   My professional mentor, Alan Weiss has always said that a consulting practice requires three things to be successful – need, competence, and passion.

   Is there a need? The answer is YES. Scott Simmonds, myself, and many others have built practices and income to support that.

Do you have competence? Only you can answer that, but if you've been successful as an agent, my guess is you are fairly competent and can improve where you're lacking.

Do you have the passion? Now this is the $64,000 question (I'm dating myself slightly). Maybe it's the $1,000,000 question! Passion for the industry, the concept, the people, and being an entrepreneur need to be present with a "no fail accepted" attitude.

If you have those three things, you have all the components that lead to being successful. The decision is ultimately yours and made on those considerations. Don't make it harder than it needs to be. Smart people make informed decisions quickly.

Note: Your answer might be NO. In fact, for most of you it probably is no. That's okay. This book is aimed at insurance agents. For most of you, this chapter may not have been applicable. However, if even 5% of you find this worthwhile, then the chapter being part of this book was a success!

2. **Decide to Move.** If the answer is yes, then move. Make the decision; plan an exit strategy for where you are currently employed; and set the stage for your next career.
3. **Get a coach or mentor.** Scott Simmonds was my first business expense at $3,500. It was a big chunk out of the gate, but maybe the most important money I spent because without his guidance, I would not have made it this far. Over the course of the past eight years, I've had multiple coaches and mentors for a variety of skills. You can't be brilliant by yourself. Find someone who has been there, done that, lived to tell about it and will help you grow. You need someone who will tell you the truth, even if it hurts. Heck, every great athlete like Tiger Woods, Kobe Bryant, and Tom Brady has coaches. You need one, too (especially at the beginning).
4. **Start making lists of everyone you know,** so you can hit the ground running. This list will be critical for gaining referrals, and building a pipeline.

There is much more, but I won't include them here. This book is about helping agents and I know this section will be important to those of you who will consider consulting. Once you've gone through Step 4, you will need to contact someone like me for help on the next steps!

Now, back to our regular program…

Chapter 12

Looking in the Crystal Ball

Thriving out of change

The insurance industry is notorious for reacting to change slowly – really slowly. While some of the change brought about by technology seems as obvious as a ham sandwich, the ultra conservative approach by the insurance empire cronies has turned it into a slow cooked roast. In the past few years, some of them have picked up the pace. I've seen the most dramatic change come in personal lines and life insurance. The rest of the lines are lagging, but they will eventually catch up.

Let's be fair, insurance agents aren't much better. In an age where web sites are the front door to your agency, many agents have hung up a "Gone Fishing" sign. Over 90% of agency web sites are boring, outdated, unimaginative, and hard to navigate. Other than that, they are fine. I still find agents who don't use voice mail, refuse to learn how to text, and believe that the best way to build their book of business is by being the cheapest option. These folks will soon go the way of the Tyrannosaurus Rex, (All of these people I run into that reject technological advances are men. Women tend to be sharper, more sophisticated, and more eager to learn than us. They undoubtedly won't get stuck in the tar pits).

Change is inevitable and the industry has seen a lot of it over the past few years. Company and agency mergers, online sales, reduced commissions, and banks getting into the business are only a few.

This chapter will pull out the crystal ball and attempt to predict what the future has in store for the insurance industry. *Change always means opportunity*. Will you die, survive, or thrive out of that change? Let's find out!

You might be in danger if...

...You don't understand how to improve relationships through technological advancement.

I've always been a fan of comedian Jeff Foxworthy. His comedic shtick, *"You Might be a Redneck If…"* is an American classic, and he now hosts a show called *Are You Smarter Than a 5th Grader* that seems to go hand in hand with the whole "redneck" principle.

> *Definition of Redneck:* Some of you reading this book in either English or some other language may not be familiar with the term "redneck." In its simplest form, a redneck refers to a Southern man in the United States who toils in the white hot sun every day working on the farm, in the fields, and on the roads. They wear shirts without collars and eschew sunscreen, so their necks over time turn the color of burnt red. Hence, the redneck. Over the years, this has come to be a playful moniker implying that rednecks "ain't very smart." While nothing could be further from the truth, real life rednecks like Mr. Foxworthy perpetuate the image through their comedy.

I've slightly altered the line to use "danger" instead of redneck. I couldn't seem to find an acceptable substitute and since I am no longer an agent, probably am outside my bounds. Feel free to figure one out for yourself!

As an insurance agent of any line of business or method of delivery, you are in danger of becoming defunct in the future world of insurance if you're not smart. Take this quick test and see if you recognize yourself. Each YES is worth 1 point, and each NO is worth zero. I am keeping it simple to avoid having you run to your nearest 5th-grader! Score yourself honestly and see what you find in the scoring legend below it:

1. I update and revise my agency web site annually. YES / NO
2. My clients have the ability to "chat" with my team on the web page. YES / NO
3. I create 'Just in Time" communications options for my clients. YES / NO
4. Clients can access their agents through a direct phone line. YES / NO
5. I send out electronic notices via email and text. YES / NO
6. I "touch" my client at least six times per year. YES / NO

7. I have an agency policy on minimum call and email return times. YES / NO

8. I offer services other than placement of insurance coverage. YES / NO

9. I try cutting edge practices, even if at a financial investment and risk. YES / NO

10. I employ the use of videoconferencing and virtual meetings to increase the quality of communications and marketing reach. YES / NO

Scoring:

9-10	Rock Star Legend
6-8	All-Star
4-5	Average Joe (on the danger line of obscurity)
1-3	Grab your waders. The tar pits are around the corner

I began with relationships because no matter how dynamic we become as a planet with technology (and I wager we are in for even greater advances), business will always be about relationships. The key is that now there is a greater expectation from those you have relationships with, and those you want to have better relationships with. Their assumption is that you are keeping up with the pack at a minimum, and cutting edge at a maximum. If you don't at least stay rooted in between those two assumptions, you won't need to worry about the rest of this chapter.

Mergers and acquisitions

If you've been in this industry as long or longer than I have, you'd have to admit that the increase of mergers and acquisitions in insurance is significantly more than ever. As Earl Bell noted in Chapter 10 on agency perpetuation, mergers and acquisitions are on the rise and will continue to be for economic and practical reasons. When you throw in the Baby Boomer factor, well…you're facing more change rather than less.

Why is this important to you? Simple. If you're oblivious to the change around you, the impact on you is akin to being blindsided by a blitzing linebacker from behind. You end up with a fumbled ball, a turnover, and a doozie of a headache. The best thing you can do is shore up your protection through knowledge, skill, and cunning.

The Blind Side: For the benefit of my non-North American friends, allow me to give a brief definition of an American football reference. Our quarterback is the guy who drops back and throws the football. The linebacker is a large mass of humanity that runs faster than a speeding bullet and can just knock buildings down rather than scale them. The visual is the poor quarterback (no eyes in the back of his head) getting driven into the ground from behind without knowledge of the impending collision. The ball goes flying (fumble) and the linebacker's teammates on defense scoop it up (turnover). This all bodes ill for the quarterback and offense, as does blindly playing the insurance game without the requisite "protection."

Here is what you need to know about mergers and acquisitions AND why they are important to you and your client. The ability to protect yourself will allow you to play that next "down."

- **Know what's going on in the industry.** It's easier than ever. Subscribe to industry newsletters, social media, or push notifications to stay apprised of developments, rumors, and innuendos. By the way, if the term "push notification" is new to you, it's time to join us in this century.
- **Strategize on what mergers and acquisitions in the industry mean to your agency**. Is it one of your company carriers? Are you better or worse off? What can you do to assure that it's the former?
- **Communicate with employees and customers**. When the whole AIG mess was in full swing, I found that there was a reticence by agents to talk much about it. The vacillation about names and constant news created more uncertainty. There is nothing wrong with saying you don't have an answer, but at the least communicate what you do know.
- **Make assumptions**. What is coming down the pike in your area? Could your competition be improving itself through M & A? If so, what does that mean for you?
- **Don't be an ostrich**. Don't keep your head in the sand because you don't want to know the news. I still see people who just go about their business with heads down and focused only on them. The problem is that in that position, you may run into something big that hurts you!

- **What are your options?** We spent an entire chapter discussing exit strategies. This is part of the overall process of determining if mergers and acquisitions are in your future.

Twenty-five years ago, people would have scoffed had you suggested that by the year 2020, there would only be three major newspapers left in print in the United States – *The Wall Street Journal*, *The New York Times*, and *USA Today*. Today, that comment doesn't seem so far fetched. In fact, consider that my prediction! The newspaper industry's inability to cope with (and actually believe) that a centuries-old institution could evaporate in a decade has led to their demise. Do you recall one of the earliest chapters in this book chronicling the history of insurance? Believe me, the industry will eventually go the same route if nobody bothers to notice.

- National brokers that are publicly owned are being much more aggressive in seeking out smaller agencies to purchase. Local area presidents and executives in these companies are being evaluated on their ability to scoop up agencies over selling insurance. As I noted earlier, I believe it just might be the quickest and most efficient way to build their book of business and leverage with company carriers.
- Small hometown agencies are making alliances in an effort to stave off larger suitors. In order to stay competitive with markets in the independent agent system, it has become increasingly important to stay competitive in increasing their own leverage with company carriers.
- Insurance companies feeling the pinch of competition and bottom line numbers are also opting for security. Who would have ever thought 30 years ago that Safeco would be purchased, or that Travelers and St. Paul would join forces in an effort to survive?
- Technology and aggressive marketing by national powerhouses have forced many company carriers and small agents to decide whether they can compete in this new "branding" environment.

All that being said, I am not suggesting that the sky is falling down on the small insurance agents and regional carriers. Actually, I am implying that this might be the best time to be in this position. The 21st Century requires you to be better branded than ever. The good news is that technology allows that and you are in a position to be more nimble and clever. This means you have to be smart, sophisticated, creative, and aggressive. Many of the recommendations and strategies you've read in this book will help you with that. In the end, the new leader of the insurance world might just be the agent that can prove that bigger isn't better and why!

Captives, pools, and self-funding

Many of you reading this are in the commercial insurance, benefits, and workers compensation world. The increase in captive insurance, risk pools, and self-funded programs is on the rise. At the end of 2011, there were nearly 6,000 captive insurers in the United States, which marks a growing trend as the Affordable Care Act and other legislation force premiums up in conventional programs.

For the sake of all our readers, let's do a quick a definition of these three alternative insurance programs:

Captive insurance

An insurance company formed by a non-insurance entity and established for the primary purpose of insuring all or part of the risk of its owners.

Example

A large seafood manufacturer decides that they understand the complexity of their General Liability and Workers Compensation risk better than conventional carriers. They believe they are being overcharged on premiums and can do a better job themselves on the risk transfer, loss control, and claims management. They form their own insurance company (now available at 30 states near you in the USA) for the sole purpose of the insuring their risk in these two lines of coverage. In essence, they become their own insurance company. The beauty of this process is that they only need to do this for the lines of coverage they want to. They may be quite satisfied with the Commercial Auto and Property and will leave that to conventional suppliers. This form of risk transfer is most common with General Liability, Workers Compensation, and Benefits.

Pools

An organization of insurers or reinsurers through which particular types of risk are underwritten with premiums, losses, and expenses shared in agreed ratios.

Example

A number of school districts in a state join forces to pool their resources to insure themselves. Unlike a captive, they hire a third-party administrator (aka TPA) and an insurance company to underwrite their risk as a whole. The pool members pay premiums, pay claims, and pay expenses based on their experience as a whole. As with captives, they believe they are better able to manage the entire loss and claims process and pay less premium by doing this themselves. They just don't have the individual financial firepower to pull off being on their own as captives are. So they band together and literally pool their resources for the benefit of each other. These pools most commonly all are part of a similar industry (e.g. school districts, municipalities) and have a shared experience and exposure.

Self-funding

The decision to retain some layer of primary coverage and to maintain some degree over the claims process.

Many businesses are large enough to take what might be considered a gargantuan deductible. They aren't in a position (or don't want) to form their own insurance company. They don't have similar industry pals to share and pool resources. Yet they desire to reduce insurance premiums and gain more control over the risk management and claims process. The other popular option is to "self-fund," or what might colloquially be termed "self insure." The organization sets a very high limit before any insurance or reinsurance comes into play. It might be in the tens of millions of dollars potentially. They take the lead on everything under the insurance limit, and save large sums of money on having the ultimately high deductible. In essence, they are truly paying for the insurance themselves and reinsuring for catastrophe.

If you're an agent, you need to be aware of the existence of these risk transfer options, whether you utilize them or not. Why?

1. You might need to write one at some point of your career. You just never know. Having a basis of understanding will make you more credible, even if you need to get help.

2. You might need to refer it out to someone else. Sometimes the best thing to do to help a client is send them away. Don't get in over your head. That is always bad for your client and for you. Or, you might be helping them with another line of insurance (personal) and can offer them a referral to a colleague that does commercial. You look like the hero. Again, a simple awareness will help you help them.

3. You might find this as an option for your career. This is a growing field and experts are needed. Maybe that's you. This might springboard you into a role of advisor and expert.

4. Sheer credibility. Your clients and prospects assume that you are intelligent in all aspects of insurance. While you might specialize in life or personal insurance, the inference is that you have credible knowledge of the industry as a whole. And they are correct….you should.

The concept of alternative ways to fund risk (insurance) is a "crystal ball thing." It is happening now and I predict will only intensify as business owners of all sizes become increasingly frustrated with rising premiums and frustration in the claims process. I have even seen captive options available for smaller businesses on a limited basis. Expect to see this more often and be prepared to respond.

Global insurance

We have spent a lot of time discussing technology in this book. The topic of the growing digital world we live in has covered marketing, communications, relationship building, time management, life balance, and metrics creation just to name a few. Let's add one more for good measure!

Companies that you insure are now doing business across the planet. That means their insurance exposures have grown both physically and from a technological standpoint. The individual people you insure are traveling to far-off lands, are working and living in different continents, and have personal insurance needs like no other time in history. Insuring a global exposure for businesses and individuals is going to eventually become more streamlined and common. That doesn't mean it comes without bumps in the road!

The vast majority of you reading this book probably have not had to deal with this global issue from a commercial insurance perspective. However every single one of you is affected in some way. Think about your own personal situation and how insurance is needed. Let's just use me as an example…

Earlier, I told the story of when I travelled to Bogota, Colombia, to give a speech. I ended up staying 10 days visiting family and enjoying the country. There are obvious insurance issues that can come to the forefront. They might include life, travel, and health insurance. However I found other things during my trip that upon further analysis are worth mentioning:

- My flight from Seattle went first to Atlanta where I connected to Bogota. As I was relaxing on the initial part of my final leg to South America, the flight attendant came by and asked what I wanted as a beverage. Knowing that I was not driving the plane, I opted for a cocktail. As I began pulling my credit card out, she stopped me and said that on international flights alcoholic drinks were complimentary. I don't do much international traveling and this was delightful news to hear. I enjoyed my drink, my flight, and later my car service ride to my hotel.

Question: Alcohol can be a large part of any international travel – business or pleasure. How does your liquor liability respond for your clients in other countries? Are there territorial limitations? What about bad behavior (e.g. driving while intoxicated)?

- I mention that I had a car service pick me up. That's not the case for a large number of both business and personal travelers.

  Question: As your insured rents a car in a foreign country and drives off to destinations unknown, what are the rules and regulations in that country? How does your policy respond, if at all? Do you educate your insureds on protocol when traveling, or do they need to figure it out on their own?

- I stayed at a very posh hotel for a couple days while in Bogota. The Hotel Sofitel attracts diplomats, ambassadors, and other big shots. The Sofitel is an international chain of luxury hotels all over the world.

  Question: What international exposures do they face with regard to employees, property, liability, and employment practices liability? If you're the agent, what challenges do you face in risk management and insurance placement?

- I spoke at the Bogota Sheraton for the event. Executives from all over South America converged just to hear me speak (well and for other things too, I suppose). The venue was decked out for the guests and we as presenters were well taken care of. The amenities included a wonderful food service for lunch and snacks.

  Question: What coverage did I have for my laptop and other business materials while there? What if I had an allergic reaction to the food? What if I was injured on the drive to and from my hotel? These sound like basic insurance issues you deal with all of the time, yet when your client is outside the country, how do they change? Heck, they don't even bother to tell you when they are gone, so it's hard to advise them. You only find out when you see their vacation pictures posted on Facebook!

- Colombia has long had a bad reputation for travelers due to the drug and mafia activity. That was very true in the 1980s and 1990s. The past decade has seen a resurgence in the country and much of the problems eradicated. Because of this, and due to the lack of an accent as compared to other countries, Colombia has become one of the hot spots for multinational companies to open call centers and locations.

  Question: While violent activity has been greatly minimized, Bogota and other large international cities are subject to violent crime. What insurance risk does that pose for your business and personal clients. Regardless of their location and purpose for being out of the country, even traveling to "safe" places like Europe is more risky. As the world becomes more global economically, this threat will continue to rise.

I could spend several pages giving you other examples, but I think you get my point. International travel and commerce have exposures, hazards, and perils just like those you find in your own country. The challenge is how do you best take care of your clients and their insurance needs if they don't even tell you they need you?

Here is a quick checklist for you to consider using with your clients, regardless of your line of business. Obviously, if you work with multinational companies and executives regularly, you will be more concerned with protections like kidnap and ransom, cyber crime, and workers compensation. But for even the small town personal lines customer service agent, these simple checklist questions will go far in helping you better protect your clients from facing a nasty uncovered claim situation.

(*Note*: You will quickly realise that this checklist is best used on an annual review of coverages – personal, commercial, and more. If you're not doing some level of this review, then you leave yourself wide open for a whopper of an Errors & Omissions claim!)

1. **Do you plan to travel internationally for business or pleasure this year?** I know that even in my Rotary Club, up to 15% of the members travel outside the country every year. That number is increasing as the economy has improved and business opportunities become more available. The affirmative answers to this question will increase. By the way, the positive response leads to a whole slew of questioning that includes car rentals, medical insurance, travel insurance, and business property, to name just a few. Don't be afraid to ask questions.

2. **When was the last time you had your life insurance reviewed (personal)?** Shouldn't you ask this question every year? Yes. But it adds more when you consider travel exposures, and I mean more than just planes. We must also consider the other modes of transport while people are away – automobiles, trains, light rail, subways, and rickshaws.

   One of the worst moments I ever had as an agent came when one of my clients and his wife took off for Miami to follow the local college football team on a road trip (although Miami and Seattle might seem to be in a different country from distance, they're not. It still is a valuable story!). My client and his wife were a young couple. He had been able to buy a franchise auto parts store at an early age. They had just had their first child when this opportunity for a cool trip came up. I had been on "Scott" for the past year to buy life insurance, even for just business considerations. Since the birth of their child, I continued my exhortations but to no avail. Eventually, I just stopped asking.

   During the trip, disaster struck. The sponsors of this trip had offered a helicopter ride to a remote Mexican island as an experience. The plane loaded up with about a dozen people and took off. Something terrible happened and the plane crashed, killing everyone on board. As you might imagine, it was headline news back home. I remember watching the late news before heading to bed when this report broke. All I could think was, "This is exactly the type of adventure Scott and his wife would be on. Oh my God, could they be one of the lost?"

   The station said a list of all who lost their lives was on their web site. I ran to my computer, turned it on, and fumbled through the whole *dial-up process* (my how times have changed). As the screeching of the dial up rang in my ears, the pit in my stomach grew bigger. I could replay every life insurance conversation I had with Scott over the past year, and saw his 2-month-old daughter being without any provisions. When I finally got the list up online, I was relieved to NOT see their names. For all my relief for that, there were still names that other people were now in shock and mourning over, including several from my hometown.

   You might say that story applies to life insurance at any time, not just globally. You're right, yet shortsighted if you commit to that point.

Travel and mobility around the globe increase the risk, even if it is just slightly.

There never is a bad time to use a story like mine to remind your clients about the importance of coverage, and to educate them on safety.

3. **Is your business selling or buying outside the country?** This question is certainly for you commercial insurance agents. However, just because you deal in solely small commercial doesn't mean the answer is going to be NO. Many small businesses do business outside their country. I have a client who is a jeweler in a town of about 6,000, yet he does business outside the United States. The implications for him can range from minor to serious depending on the situation. Be prepared to advise a client.

4. **Does your business sell or receive income from the Internet?** Remember that the www prefix translates into "World Wide Web." That means sales and income could be coming from anywhere in the world. Is this a problem? Maybe not, but you need to know.

5. **Do you have any family members (insureds) that live abroad?** From a personal lines perspective, your client may have children that are still considered part of the house living in other countries. When our oldest daughter was a sophomore in college, she spent a semester studying in Austria with her school. She lived a more Spartan life for those 3-4 months, but she did take personal property, a laptop, and other things. In this case, I needed to ensure that coverage is in place just as if she was living in her dorm room. Your clients may not even think about this.

   It doesn't only have to be college kids, either. There are many high school exchange programs and kids are leaving for up to 12 months. How is their personal property and health insurance covered?

The crystal ball is clear. Being prepared to be knowledgeable about global insurance and the consequences of it is important for you as an insurance professional. At the most, you might find this to be a career path. At the least, take a few classes for continuing education and be prepared to sound astute if you're ever asked a question.

Bottom line

In a very volatile and ever changing world, insurance can be really hard to figure out. Trying to use a crystal ball might be as effective as trying to cage a roomful of cats. What you can be assured of is that change is guaranteed and being alert and aware for changes will only enhance your career.

Chapter 13

Get a Life

How to make sure you don't go off the deep end without a life jacket

You don't have a professional life and a personal life. You have a life. This bit of wisdom comes to me from my professional mentor, Alan Weiss. He's right. In today's world of technology, instant and ubiquitous access, and ever demanding careers and families, you can't take one life out of another.

I'm a school board director for my hometown school district and one of the topics we always need to explain to people is how the operational levy works. In our district, this levy that is funded by taxpayer dollars accounts for about 23% of our overall general fund budget. We exhaust a lot of time, money, and effort into putting together elaborate graphs and charts showing where the taxpayer dollars are allocated in the budget. It's as if we need to placate all those people who are interested in 1. 7% of their tax dollars going to the afternoon snack at Pearson Elementary. These are four-year levies, which means that over the course of that time, what you thought the money might get used for is completely different to what it is required to be used for.

The reality is that all that money that accounts for 23% of the budget gets dumped in a vat with the other income we receive from the state. It ends up funding everything from teacher pay, to athletics, to special education, and to music. Everything. What I tell people most simply is that once all that money gets dumped into the vat, it can't help but be mixed into the entire amount. It's like adding sugar into a pie. It may be only a fraction of the ingredients, but it finds its way to 100% of the pie. The levy dollars end up at some fractional level funding everything.

That's how your life works. You have your insurance career and that seeps into your personal time. You can't partition your family out of your daily thoughts as you head to an appointment. Your kid's soccer matches are often at 2:00 pm and your emails sometimes gets returned at 11:30 pm.

Life and work balance is a myth. What we all really do is manage and prioritize our time, our thinking, our activities, and our behaviors. In the insurance industry, this managing process can be taxing and overwhelming. If not done well, it will lead to guilt, anxiety, poor health, and less than adequate performance. My simple solution for you is this – Get a Life! In this chapter, we will discuss strategies that lead to:

- Improved time management skills
- Better delegating
- Leveraging technology, and
- Setting real priorities.

Maximizing how you manage that life will actually change it for the better, and for good.

Time is on my side

Time (like money) is not a resource issue, it's a priority issue. We all get 24 hours in the day. It doesn't matter if you're Stephen Hawking, Bill Gates, Lady Gaga, or the President of the United States. We all get the same time. The difference between the most successful people and those that struggle with getting things accomplished lies with how they prioritize that time. My work with coaching agency owners and producers always starts with examining how they prioritize their time. Why don't we start there with you, too!

Exercise

1. Take a sheet of paper (that's right, not electronic, real paper) and a pen, and chart out a simple time journal.
2. The journal should be metered out in 15-minute increments for the time you are awake during the day.
3. Chart what you do in each of those 15 minutes and be honest. For instance, as I am typing on my computer for this book you're reading, I would allocate four 15-minute segments because I write for an hour a day. If you take 30 minutes to read and respond to emails, then mark two spots. Round off to the nearest mark. This data is only for you, so it doesn't have to be ultra precise or perfectly neat. You're not turning this in to the teacher. It's your tool.

4. Do this for a minimum of a week and a maximum of three weeks.

5. Do not change your habits for the exercise. That will skew your results. So will reading what you do as you go. It's optimal to just chart and not assess or judge until the entire project is done. Remember, you're not sharing this with others so it's not about looking like you're Stephen Covey. This needs to be an unequivocal snapshot of you. Being "nice" to yourself will not change behaviors. Show some tough love!

Your results should be reviewed right after the project by you and by your coach or mentor. If you don't have one of those, find an unbiased, brutally candid, and willing person to help you look at your time priorities. These are the questions you should be asking yourself:

- **What are my personal and professional priorities and am I spending the bulk of my time on that?** Example – I had a coaching client who needed to professionally focus on mergers & acquisitions, hiring new producers, and "coaching up" his staff. On the personal side, he had a young family that required his time and attention. We looked at his time journal and noted that much of his time was being taken by administrative tasks, which could have been delegated to others. Which leads to the next question to ask yourself...

- **Am I doing what only I can do?** A colleague and friend of mine named Jim Hessler once addressed a group of CEOs I was leading. He said to them, "80% of your activities should be things that ***only you*** can do." This is the point I would go over the time journals and start counting. 80% has never been reached on the first attempt yet! How does yours look?

Let's examine this question a little more closely. Many of the things that you have been unwilling to give up are easily accomplished by someone else. It is baggage weighing you down. How can you be nimble with your time when you're trying to drag 100-pound luggage around with you all the time (which by the way seems to always pick up more along the way)?

Be honest about where your skills, strengths to the organization, and clear objectives are. Is making copies the best use of your time? How about sending out correspondence, or talking to the marketing rep from a company? Can someone else make the coffee?

Here is a rule of thumb: Take a look at your activity. Make a decision as to whether you are the only one that can do this, or can it be done by someone else.

If it's you, fine. If not, then you have to either delegate or train someone. Many of you resist training because you say, *"By the time I train them, I could do it myself. It's just easier for me to do it."* When you start adding up the amount of time that ends up being, it might make you sick to your stomach.

Here is an example for an agency owner with a staff of 10 people. She has two commercial producers, and the rest are service staff. Agency owners of this size think they are overwhelmed because they HAVE to wear all the hats. This is usually not the case.

Activity	Responsibility	Action
Opening company mail	NO	Delegate to receptionist
Meeting with new carrier marketing rep	NO (give them 5 minutes as a courtesy and then…)	Delegate to your producers
Financial analysis	NO	Hire a bookkeeper either internally or externally
Sales management	YES	Only you can do this at this point. Maybe in the future you can train.
Email responses	YES (but…)	Delegate items not pertaining to you to an assistant to deal with.

This list could go on and on. The moral of the story is that if you're like most people, you are reluctant to let go of some things that you believe that only you can do. With a little training, oversight or just simple abandonment, you can free up a lot of your time.

- **Am I holding appointments with myself as sacrosanct?** This was my biggest transgression. You would never cancel or postpone an appointment with a client or prospect (outside of an emergency). Yet if you are like me, it's very easy to cancel on yourself. After all, it's only you! If you can learn how to schedule appointments with yourself and commit to keeping them, you will find your projects and requirements will get done on time. You will lose all that guilt that you heap on yourself for not meeting your goals. And, you will also end up helping all those around you because what you're doing is important to their success.

Example: I've worked closely with many executives in and out of the insurance industry. A common theme is that they don't have the time to adequately kick their feet up on their desk, clasp their hands behind their head, and think. Think about their business. Strategize on how to grow, improve, and better serve clients. Why? Because of all the other "stuff" they have to deal with.

Folks, this isn't rocket science. As an agency executive or principal, you are responsible for the vision, the culture, and the strategic growth of your company or agency. People (employees, clients, families) are counting on you doing this. They need you to be strategic more than they need you to make the coffee in the morning. Pick time during the week (e.g. every Monday and Thursday morning at 8:30 for one hour), and put it in your calendar. Then block out any distractions (emails, phone calls, text messages, Angry Birds) and hold that time sacred. Do not give it away to looking at your email, catching up on work from yesterday, or searching for swizzle sticks for the coffee. This is your time for being visionary about your agency. Someone has to do it, and this is one of those things that fall in the 80%.... only you can do it.

My Seven Time Control Myths and Truths

There are time management experts and books all over the place. You can stumble over any of them surfing the Internet. Most of what they talk about is really good old common sense. Much of what you will hear from me is the same. These experts and authors are mostly all good. In fact, some are really excellent. However, instead of reading an entire book devoted to time management (which you might consider a time drain in and of itself), allow me to share my seven time control devices right here and right now in this chapter. If you commit to doing these seven behaviors well, I guarantee you will return significant time back in your day. Now start reading before you waste ay more!

Myth #1: Time is a resource issue. Truth: Time is a priority issue

You read this earlier in the chapter. Consider yourself getting hit over the head with a 2x4 for good measure to cement this point! We all get the same amount of time in a day. It doesn't matter who you are. There is a limited and known quantity of resource, so it automatically becomes a priority.

Myth #2: You can manage time. Truth: You can't manage time. You can only direct your priorities.

This carries through with Myth #1. You can't manage something that just keeps going no matter what. You direct your priorities to meet your desires in how you spend time. There is no good or bad. This is based on how you want to spend your time.

One of my colleagues, Libby Wagner, has posited that we spend 90,000 hours at work in a career. 90,000. That can be a seemingly overwhelming number to contemplate. How do you want to spend that time? Or, maybe the better questions is – can you, through better time direction, actually spend less than that and increase what is really true wealth, your discretionary time?

Myth #3: Other people dictate your time. Truth: You allow other people to dictate your time.

Someone else's emergency isn't necessarily your emergency. Just because you have that wicked "open door policy," doesn't mean it's analogous to Grand Central Station. My guess is that other people bring you their crises to quickly get them off their plate and add them to yours. You need to control and educate others on what is acceptable, what the definitions of important and urgent are, and when you can be interrupted. You control your environment whether you believe it or not. You might just have to get tough though.

Myth #4: Technology has increased your workload and time burden. Truth: You have allowed technology to tax your time.

Technology is your friend. However, it's one of those friends that if you get too attached to will bilk you for every minute you have. However, if you can control this relationship, technology might be the very best friend you have.

Myth #5: I have to separate work time from personal time to be happy. Truth: You can't be happy unless you're flexible enough to direct time your way.

You won't believe how many times I've heard this one. In all my years in business, this might be the biggest myth of them all. Granted, when we were less digital it was easier to do. But, today, it makes no sense and is even counterproductive.

Consider this. How much time to you waste catching up on things? If you were on vacation for a week, you'd have just under a gazillion emails to look at. How about instead you pick up your email three times a day (morning noon and evening)? You spend 15 minutes prioritizing, culling through, deleting, and delegating those emails. When you get back to work after your vacation, you have less stress and more time back in your pocket because your email is ready to roll on a current state.

Myth #6: I can't eliminate anything from my day. Truth: You can eliminate almost anything, but you choose not to.

You may have said this at some point in your life. I know I have. The truth is that most of what you do can be delegated to someone else who will undoubtedly do it better and faster than you; or maybe it shouldn't be done at all. We all carry baggage around that eats away at our day. One of two things will happen – either you do the extraneous work to the detriment of your overall minutes, or the task falls through those cracks that we always speak of and you get to play the guilt game.

Take a hard look at what you do daily. Is this your best use of time? Is it what you like to do? Is it advancing you or your business? If the answer to these questions is NO, then you have some baggage to heave off the train.

Myth #7: I don't have enough time. Truth: You do have enough time. The choice is yours.

Everyone has enough time. Nobody in history ever got more or less. If Thomas Edison, Albert Einstein, and Groucho Marx could work around it, so can you. The biggest roadblock unfortunately is staring at you in the mirror. You don't think you have enough time because you're falling victim to the first six myths. Like I told you a couple of pages ago – take care of these simple myths and your time will come flowing to you like you hit the jackpot in Las Vegas.

Seven Technology Tips

A different chapter in this book discusses technology as it relates to your career and leveraging it for acquiring and retaining business. This section on technology is to help you leverage technology in your behaviors (both professional and personal) to save you valuable time, reduce frustration, and be far more productive. Like My Seven Myths and Truths you just read, I have Seven Technology Tips to help you maximize your day and have to more discretionary time.

1. **Cell He#%&*@*** – If you have a little blue blinking device affixed to your ear constantly, you have a serious problem. If you're like me, you've called someone on their cell phone, only to have them answer and whisper, "I'm in a meeting. Can I call you back?" If you're in a meeting, don't answer the phone! Why are we humans so attached to answering every phone call the second it comes in regardless of the task we are doing?

   The problem is that when you answer the phone, you're distracting yourself from whatever task you were doing. That might be a meeting, driving, working on a project, or even your down time for lunch. The solution is to only use your phone as an outgoing device. That's right, ignore the incoming calls and allow them to go to voice mail. Here are the reasons why:

   - You won't distract yourself from whatever priority you had set. What you're doing when that call comes in was probably on your calendar (or should have been) or is requiring your full attention (driving and walking). This allows you to complete your task and be more efficient.
   - You can check all your voice mails at once and return the calls when you have more information. People may leave you clues as to why they called and you can better prepare for your response.
   - Rarely is a call a life or death matter. Sometimes they are urgent, yet rarely are they emergencies. You calling back in less than 60 minutes is adequate 99% of the time.
   - Most importantly, you (not your phone) are choosing your time priority. It's showing you that you can take your life back!

Note: I do make a few exceptions. The nursing facility my mother is in is a priority. When they call, it's usually on an urgent or highly important level. Clients understand that. My wife and kids text me, as I will usually see that first. This allows me to take a quick peek and determine urgency. 99% of the time, it's not urgent and I can respond as if returning a voice mail. We also have a deal if they call back-to-back then this represents a 911 call (I had to work on my kids with the definition of "emergency"). I've set guidelines with family as to how I will respond to them, knowing that they are in the big scheme my most important priorities. You must have a similar group of people, be it family or even VIP clients. You can set up the same type of system with them. Communication is pivotal to achievement.

2. **In Sync** – Technology has made it very simple to sync your life. I am an evangelist for Apple products. For me and my life, they have worked the best, so I own only Apple products. Part of the attraction is the ease in syncing my life. I can, without any "connections", sync my contacts, my calendar, my communications (email and text), my entertainment, and my work without having to do anything. The Cloud handles all of it and my adding something to one devise, updates all the others.

   Why would someone not do this? Because there is a fear of the unknown, of admitting being unenlightened, that they will abuse the process, and a general fear that by making that leap they will forever be tethered to technology. In the meantime, they end up not using something that is ubiquitously available, inordinately inexpensive, and easily accessible.

   Make your life easier. Use whatever disciplines work for you to avoid abuse of time. By syncing all your work, your contacts, your communications, and your calendars, you are less likely to miss an important event or meeting. You are more likely to be on time, prepared, and professional. I would have thought by this time that the art and science of syncing would be as commonplace as the syncing of brushing and flossing your teeth daily. That being said, according to my dentist, the flossing doesn't get synced as often as it should either!

3. **Where am I?** – I remember being an agent in the 1990s and each year purchasing a voluminous book published by Rand McNally called the *Thomas Guide*. This book was a necessity for anyone doing any amount

of business travel. For those of you too young to remember it, the guide was based on whatever area you wanted and drilled down with each age every nook, street, and cranny of the cities, towns, and rural locations you might need to travel to. It needed to be updated regularly as construction would make the current book obsolete quickly.

To make things more cumbersome, you needed to read the map while you were driving. No amount of preparatory work was going to tattoo the information in your cerebral cortex. The real danger (and remember we are risk experts) came in trying to find out where Smith Street and 21st intersected.

As I drive around listening to Sophia (the name with which I've anointed the female voice in my mobile device) tell me how to get to anywhere I want to go, I think back on those days and chuckle. Maps that you were unable to re-fold ever again have gone the way of the dodo bird. The bulky *Thomas Guides* that I mention in my story are now computerized. Getting from your current location to Timbuktu is easily mapped and metered out (this journey will require a water passage for most of you). Why is it then that I still hear business professionals lament the fact they are late because they got lost? In this era, how can it be that someone doesn't have updated technology?

Look, you are a professional. If you're not already doing so, invest in some type of Global Positioning System (GPS). For goodness sakes, your smart phone has the capability and if it doesn't, get a new one. This is more than being professional to your clients. This is about your frustration, anxiety, and time. I remember the threat of being late, the anxiety of being lost, and the danger of being in an accident always impacted my own "life balance" when I was in that situation. It will for you, too. Take advantage of the advances of "just in time" technology and get the best GPS you can find. It will improve your stress level and get you to where you need to be.

4. **Entertainment Ethos** – I love television. I have since I was a kid watching the *Justice League of America* and *Loony Tunes* on the "tube." (Funny – I don't believe "tubes" even exist anymore for TVs.) Television for me is still one of my biggest forms of relaxation. Yours may be different. We all have different forms of entertainment we need to help create good mental health and balance.

Note – In this example, entertainment means television, music, and other platforms that you do from home to kick back and relax.

If you're like me, you may enjoy sitting around the house late at night before you go to bed with your significant other watching TV or a movie with some popcorn and a glass of wine. In the old days, you were chained to watch whatever was being televised. Even with the ability to record on VHS, it was often an onerous task that required some degree in engineering to "tape" a 60-minute episode of *Hill Street Blues*. Today, you are in charge of what you watch and when you watch it. You are literally the "on demand" chief of your house (or at least second in command).

Smart televisions, cable, satellite, and low cost subscription services like Netflix and Amazon abound. They can be wirelessly transferred to your big screen from your computer to watch your favorite shows when relaxation is at a premium for you. Why do I make such a big deal of this? Because I have opined earlier in this chapter that time is a priority issue. You get to prioritize what you want to do, and if relaxing and closing out the evening watching your favorite show is to be between 9:00 and 11:00 pm, then you should be able to watch whatever it is that makes you happy. Part of a really healthy life is being able to stop and force yourself to relax. You can easily make that process simpler.

Okay, a quick comment for my non-television watchers. You may do something else that relaxes you at night. It might be music, crossword puzzles, or knitting. Do it. That's the crux. I just know that the majority of people I talk with like television as their diversion, so I offer ways to maximize that here.

5. **Text Mania** – I still remember the first text message I ever received and sent. I was in Steubenville, Ohio, with my oldest daughter, Mindy. I was dropping her off at school for her freshman year of college in 2007. The text identification was just a cell number and it was about someone having a baby. I remember asking Mindy what to do with it. I could almost hear her eyes rolling as I stared at the phone screen. My response was a classic – "Who is this?" The text came from a former coach on my basketball staff and it was on a group message about her having a baby. Her first baby and my first text. For my part, a monster had been created!

Today, I text a lot more, and it's not just for personal use. Easily 50% of my text messages are for business reasons, and it may be more than that if I actually charted it. Texting is not a "kid thing." It's a very reliable, fast, and efficient way to communicate information. It will also make your life easier.

Consider the time you spend sending and waiting for emails. My guess is that the majority of emails are nothing more than informational, rather than "contractual." Allow me to explain.

Contractual emails are those that deal with issues that are lengthy, need to be kept, and are weighty. For example – proposals, certificates of insurance, binders, claims communications, endorsements, relational discussions, and company carrier information. These are like the old school hard copies that were filed in gargantuan file cabinets that took up half your office space. Today, they are still as necessary but can be kept in miniature form on your server.

Informational emails at least for me are more frequent and timely. They include (but of course are not limited to) – confirmation of meetings/calls, availability requests, running early or late notices, urgent call notifications, and picking up toilet paper (that's from my wife). These messages tend to get read first, responded to first, and (importantly for you) are an easier access to your clients (if agreeable with them).

Bottom line – Make excellent use of technology and texting. Use it with your support staff, your company underwriters and marketing people, your clients, and your family. I've found my proliferating use of text messaging has made my life much easier through quicker and timelier information gathering.

Note: As I've always preached to my kids, texting is NOT a relationship tool. It is not how you enhance a relationship with a prospect, nor is it how you augment one with your client. It is, however, an excellent way to propagate information in a way that will boost your professionalism and value to your client.

Oh...by the way. Don't walk and text. My daughter did that on campus and walked right into a bike rack. The bloody and bruised lip in first period taught her a lesson. We as adults might actually ***really*** hurt ourselves!

---

6. **Storage Wars** – You may be familiar with the cable television reality show bearing this name. Professional storage mongers get a glimpse of a packed storage unit that has gone delinquent and is now owned by the storage unit owner. The mongers determine how badly they want the contents of this unit and then enter into an auction. To the winner go the spoils, good or bad.

   I'd often wished that my home's junk could be just auctioned off. Since most of my "stuff" hadn't been used in years, I probably didn't need it anymore. When I recently went through the job of digging through said "stuff," I found an array of items I had at one point frantically looked for, had to purchase a new one of since I didn't know where it was, or been inordinately frustrated or angry about. I've got a colleague who is an expert in helping you clean and organize your life in an orderly fashion (not a career I would be savvy at). She says that reducing just the pure stress of looking for items when they are most needed is worth its weight in gold.

   Our job in the insurance industry is brimming with data storage. We have loads of client and prospect information, photos of insured locations, company carrier information, personal information, employee files, and proposals. This list is only the tip of the iceberg. The problem arises when you can't find that important email or client information that you need to have right now. Don't tell me that this hasn't happened to you. It has happened (and still does) with all of us.

   The solution is exceptional storage and document file management. Regardless of your role in the agency or company, you have important documents, emails, and other correspondence that you need to find eventually. That needs to be readily accessible through ***proper labeling and filing*** (one of my first valuable lessons years ago on this subject). You need to learn how to effortlessly find things in your computer's **search function**. This was also a trial and error experience for me that I wish I had been better trained at earlier. Finally, you should be saving all your needed emails in ***file folders***. File folder management is an art in and of itself. Your agency should be using the same system and file names.

   Bottom line – if you add up all the time you waste in searching for things that should be at your fingertips, I bet you could recover a full week of work and lose a lot less gray hair! A balanced life is one that maximizes time and decreases stress. Mastering the "storage wars" will greatly assist you in this quest.

7. **Don't Unplug** – If you're like me, you might have friends that often write on Facebook who they are "unplugging" for their vacation or even just the weekend. They are getting away from it all. Don't try to stop them or reach them. Sounds good in theory, yet my experience is that it adds tremendous stress that could easily be alleviated with a little discipline.

   Consider the results of "unplugging" for a week:

   - **Email purgatory.** While some of your email may get diverted for others to handle, most if it probably needs to be addressed by you. If you never check it or handle it until you return, you might just spend the first three days back responding to email.
   - **Voice mail perdition.** The road to perdition for you might be listening to 47 voice mails that either didn't get transferred or were personal and confidential (which is most likely the case). Have fun listening and returning those calls, along with your plethora of email plus the new work stacked on your desk.
   - **Important becomes urgent.** There are some situations that are important at the outset. With the passage of time (and sometimes not much of it), urgency is the new reality. If for some reason that request never made it to you or someone covering for you then anxiety, anger, and apoplexy may be the outcome!

Let's go back to the premise that you don't have a professional life and a personal life; you have a *life*. There is now more than ever every reason to include a little of that "professional" into your "personal" to make the whole much better. What is required is discipline and I suggest that this is what scares most people away from doing this...they know they are likely to be undisciplined! Here is a little help from me. Practice these simple strategies and you will find that both your free time and your return time will be ameliorated.

1. **Check your email three times a day.** Take no more than 20 minutes in the morning, the afternoon, and the evening to check your email. Make conclusive decisions on what you do with each. Choose to delete, delegate, or answer and file. Period. Make sure that you don't see that email again when you return. This will prevent any *important to urgent* concerns, as well as eliminate the email purgatory.

2. **Utilize text for important issues.** Notice I didn't say urgent. Important can often turn into urgent and this is a great way to *head these off at the pass*. Text is easy and quick to respond to and won't disturb your sunbathing.

> *Head off at the pass* is a very American term meant to stop a dreadful event from occurring. In classic western movies, the "good guys" would attempt to head off the "bad guys" at the pass, to assure that they didn't make it in to the town to do their dirty work. The pass was the only route into town, so meeting them there was required, and made for great "shoot outs" loved by moviegoers of all generation!

3. **Forward your phone to your mobile device.** You don't have to answer the phone when it rings. Let it go to voice mail and return to it later. Conversely, you can delegate it to someone else to deal with in your absence and it disappears from your proverbial "plate."
4. **Check in every couple of days.** The length of your check-in doesn't need to be longer than five minutes. There is no need to exchange pleasantries for more than 15 seconds. Tell your co-workers your vacation photos are on Facebook. Get a quick update of only things that you need to know or make a quick decision on. Hang up. Simple.
5. **Don't feel guilty.** It's okay to do a little work on vacation. You have no reason to feel guilty. As long as it's not a burden, it's easy, and you enjoy doing it, do it. When you're officially working, you might leave to go watch your daughter play soccer. Insurance is a results business. Get the results and gain the freedom to unplug!

Thoughts on getting a life from Captain Jack

Final thoughts on getting a life from Captain Jack. Captain Jack is my Jack Russell terrier and he has a column in my newsletter. Not only do I listen to what my wife tells me to do, but my dog dictates to me, too. Dogs have a unique world view and Jack has taught me we would do better if we followed the lead dog sometimes. Here is one of his best. I can think of no better way to end this book than with his commentary on life.

"Humans are lousy at living a good life compared to us dogs. You worry and fret over things too much. Dogs make life and work fun (some of us do work you know). I have my own rules of engagement for dog life balance. I'm giving them to you before you go off the deep end....

Rule 1: The Yard. When I go out into *The Yard*, it's a new adventure every day. It may be the same place, but there are new smells, new adventures, and new snakes to hunt. *The Yard* is my favorite part of the day because it's the start of a new adventure in olfactory sensory overload. Humans sometimes look at the day as humdrum. Same old, same old. Boring. You should be like us. We don't care that it's the same yard. We are happy because we have a yard. You should be happy you have a new day.

Rule 2: The Walk. Dogs need to keep their physique. From what I've seen from a bunch of humans, you do, too. Dan makes sure we get out and walk even if it's wet and cold. Exercise feeds our bodies and keeps our minds sharp. If you feel good, you play (dogs and humans) and work (humans and dogs) well. Some of you are overdue for *The Walk*.

Rule 3: The Wonder. I recently saw a full moon in the back yard. Believe it or not, we dogs do get pensive in looking at the moon. It kind of looks like food. We love to learn, try things, and be curious. If you never lose your childlike wonder and love of learning and trying, you're likely to be just as happy as a dog.

Rule 4: Relax. Humans work too hard. But that's not the worst part. You work too hard and you don't relax enough. You never hear of a workaholic dog do you? Take time to relax and refresh your mind.

Rule 5: Sleep. We Jack Russell terriers live a long time because we are so good at sleeping. I read (yes dogs read...one of the mysteries you humans haven't picked up yet) that American humans are the most sleep deprived of all human nations. Maybe it's all the coffee, but why would you want to do that? I know I've heard Dan say that there is a whole bunch of research that links lack of sleep with poor productivity, health issues as you age, and a general, overall crankiness. No good can come from lack of sleep.

Take it from a dog, if you want to live a happier, healthier life where you can unleash your potential, live like us dogs. You may even find a few extra treats on your dish!"

Captain Jack (2014)

Appendix A

Dan's Checklist for Client Needs

Personal Insurance

- Homeowners/Renters
- Personal Auto
- Personal Umbrella
- Inland Marine (Jewelry/etc)
- Motorcycle/Boat/Recreational Vehicle
- Life
- Disability
- Long-Term Care
- Accident
- Individual Medical/Dental/Vision
- Pet Insurance
- Home-Based Business Exposure
- Issues related to living with significant others/partners/or roommates
- Issues related to children away from home at school
- Vacant Property or Land
- Rental Property
- Secondary Residences
- Earthquake & Flood

Commercial Insurance

- Commercial Property
- Commercial Liability

- Business Income
- Professional Liability (Errors & Omissions)
- Workers Compensation
- Technology
- Cyber Liability
- Employment Practices Liability
- Inland Marine
- Ocean Marine
- Jones Act Exposures (Longshoremen)
- Builders Risk
- Crime (Employee Dishonesty/Money & Securities)
- Pollution
- Business Income for Dependent Properties
- Directors & Officers Liability
- International Liability
- Crisis Management Expense Coverage
- Vacant Property/Land
- Group Benefits (Medical/Dental/Vision/Life/Disability)
- Kidnap & Ransom
- Key Man Life to Fund Buy-Sell Agreements
- Key Man Life to Protect Death or Disability to Key Employees
- Reputation Risk
- Liquor Liability
- Difference in Conditions (Earthquake/Flood/More)

Appendix B

Dan's Guide to Overcoming Objections

Objections shouldn't be feared. They are actually a form of interest. You need to know that objections fall into only four categories:

1. **No Time** – This is simply a technique to get you to leave. Time is a priority issue and they are telling you you're not a priority. This happens when the relationship hasn't been cultivated to a point where there is trust that you offer value. It often happens when you try to rush through the process, rather than thinking relationship first.
2. **No Money** – This is another tactic used to get rid of you. They are trying to discourage you into thinking they aren't the type of client you want. They have money they are spending on insurance. They have money to allocate to a myriad of business expenses. They don't see the value or return on investment. That's on you!
3. **No Need** – For some lines of insurance, you won't hear this because they do have a need (e.g. personal auto, commercial, workers compensation). However if you sell "discretionary" insurance (e.g. Life, Long-Term Care, Disability, Cyber Liability, Employment Practices) then you're almost assured to hear it. For these objections, neither value nor sense of urgency has been created. They don't know or understand the risk. That's on you.
4. **No Trust** – This is the granddaddy of them all. The first three objections are specious. This one is your biggest hurdle. Trust takes time, cultivation, patience, and smarts. You have to get them to a place where they believe you have their best interest at heart and you've got solutions to their problems. Trust always needs to lead or you're just a commodity broker, not a trusted advisor.

My tips and tactics for you:

1. Never lead with price. Always lead with trying to develop a relationship.
2. Provide value…lots of it. It might be your own intellectual process or your company's. Talk about improving their condition before taking their money.
3. Invite them to events that you hold for free. This is another place to provide value.
4. Talk about things other than insurance. Be an object of interest.
5. Add them to your free mailing list with their permission.
6. Be ubiquitous without haunting them.
7. Direct them to your web site, your testimonials, and to people who will give reference to your great work.

I guarantee you this...most of your competition doesn't provide this much value to their clients, which means you have an opportunity to impress. That being said, you need to do the same with your clients or else someone else who is reading this book will be on the trail to do the same for them!

Let's discuss how to convert objections into new business by using language.

(*Important Note* - Most of these tactics have been given to me by my mentor, Alan Weiss. Alan created a template for consultants to use to rebut objections and has given his blessing for me to share it with my community. If you'd like to see the entire white paper, email me at dan@weedin.com and I will send it to you)

1. Why do you feel that way? (Gets to the true cause)
2. If we resolve this, can we then proceed? (Is this the sole objection?)
3. But isn't that exactly why you need me? (The reversal approach)
4. What would satisfy you? (Make the buyer answer the objection)
5. What can we do to overcome that? (Demonstrate joint accountability)

Appendix C

Dan's 10 Best Practices for Networking Events

1. **Do your homework first**. Find out who some of the guests or attendees will be and learn a little bit about them. Be prepared to sound interesting and knowledgeable.
2. **Don't mix with people you already know**. The goal is to meet new prospective clients.
3. **Don't drink alcohol**. As much as I like a nice glass of wine, if I am working I need to be focused. (Note – if this event is a formal charity-style event where wine is available at the table, go ahead and have a glass. Avoid the bar and overindulging on the wine, though. It's never in your best interest.)
4. **Display good manners**. One thing my mother drilled into me was manners around food and a table. I didn't appreciate the significance it then, but I do now. Little things like using your fingers as a knife to scoop up food on your fork can have a detrimental effect on you!
5. **Focus on whom you're talking to**. Nothing is quite as rude as having someone staring at the person they *really* want to talk to while in conversation with you. If you need to make an exit, be gracious. Otherwise, stay in the moment.
6. **Be prepared to make a date**. It's unlikely that the place you're at is a great situation to discuss much business. Offer to meet at their office at a more appropriate time to continue discussions. Schedule the date right then and there and move on.
7. **Never sell**. Never. Networking events are filled with odious sales people trying to pitch you in elevators and bathrooms. Always stay above that fray. You're goal is to get a meeting.

8. **Set goals**. You should have a minimum and maximum expectation going in. Your minimum might be to set two appointments. If you accomplish this, it's been a success. Your maximum might be that you gain 5 new meetings. This is the time to leave quickly before your luck runs out!

9. **Hand out cards judiciously**. Remember those odious sales people that think that whoever hands out the most business cards wins? Give your card out when there is interest in the other side and/or you make an appointment.

10. **Have fun**. If you aren't having fun or don't support the cause, it shows. Go to events where the people you want to meet will be, but choose ones where you will also have a fun time. People are attracted to positive vibes, and you need to give them off.